# Shape and space

## The School Mathematics Project

CAMBRIDGE
UNIVERSITY PRESS

| **Main authors** | Stan Dolan |
| | Ron Haydock |
| | Paul Roder |
| | |
| **Contributions from** | Diana Sharvill |
| | Thelma Wilson |
| | |
| **Team leader** | Paul Roder |

The authors and publisher would like to thank the following for supplying photographs:

front cover – Ballooning by Adina Tovy, Robert Harding Picture Library; pages 17 and 42 – ZEFA Picture Library (UK) Ltd.

Cartoons by Gordon Hendry

Published by the Press Syndicate of the University of Cambridge
The Pitt Building, Trumpington Street, Cambridge CB2 1RP
40 West 20th Street, New York, NY 10011–4211, USA
10 Stamford Road, Oakleigh, Melbourne 3166, Australia

© Cambridge University Press 1993

First published 1993

Produced by Gecko Limited, Bicester, Oxon

Cover design by Iguana Creative Design

Printed in Great Britain at the University Press, Cambridge

A catalogue record for this book is available from the British Library

*Library of Congress cataloguing in publication data applied for*

ISBN 0 521 44731 3

# Contents

# **1** **Positions and polygons**

## 1.1 Loci

In this chapter you will learn how to find the **locus**, or range of possible positions, of a point. In Latin the word 'locus' means 'position'. In mathematics it refers to a set of points. Many loci are defined as the paths traced out by moving objects.

(a) A ladder is leaning against a vertical wall with its foot on horizontal ground. It then slips until it is flat on the ground. What is the locus of its mid-point?

(b) A garden sprinkler is placed on a lawn in the position shown in the diagram. The sprinkler rotates while spraying water up to a maximum distance of 5 metres.

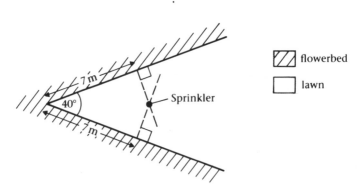

Make an accurate scale drawing and shade the part of the lawn which is being watered.

You saw in the discussion point how a locus can be:

● a set of points which form a path;

● a set of points enclosed in an area.

You can use your drawing instruments to construct other interesting loci.

*TASKSHEET  1  —  Two buoys (page 14)*

*EXAMPLE  1*

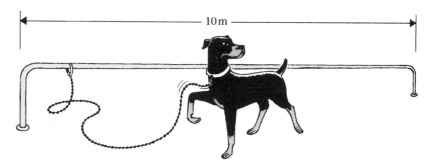

A guard-dog is tethered to a horizontal rail. The lengths of the rail and the tether are 10 m and 5 m respectively. The tether has a ring at the end which slides along the rail. Sketch the area which is guarded by the dog.

*SOLUTION*

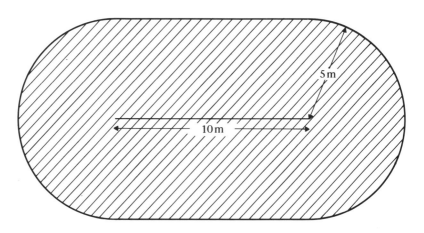

*EXAMPLE 2*

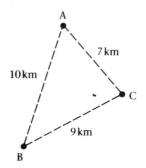

There are lighthouses at A and B and a lightship at C. A helicopter flies at $200\,\mathrm{km\,h^{-1}}$ so that at any time its distance from A is the same as its distance from B.

For how many minutes is it within 5 km of the lightship?

*SOLUTION*

The path of the helicopter can be shown on a scale drawing by constructing a line which:

- passes through the mid-point of AB;

- is perpendicular to AB.

The set of points within 5 km of C (the lightship) is represented on the diagram as the points inside a circle, drawn to the correct scale.

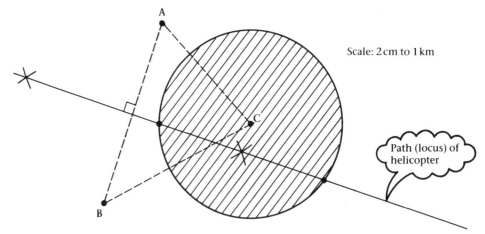

Scale: 2 cm to 1 km

Path (locus) of helicopter

The helicopter is within 5 km of the lightship when its path lies in the shaded area. The length of this path is approximately 4·7 cm when measured on the diagram, which is 9·4 km on the ground.

The helicopter travels at 200 km per hour, so the time for which it is within 5 km of the lightship is given by:

Time = distance ÷ speed
$$= 9\!\cdot\!4 \div 200 \;= 0\!\cdot\!047 \text{ hours}$$
$$= 0\!\cdot\!047 \times 60 = 2\!\cdot\!82 \text{ minutes.}$$

So the helicopter is within 5 km of the lightship for just under 3 minutes.

In solving example 2 you needed to know the locus of points equidistant from two fixed points, as well as the locus of points within a certain distance of a fixed point.

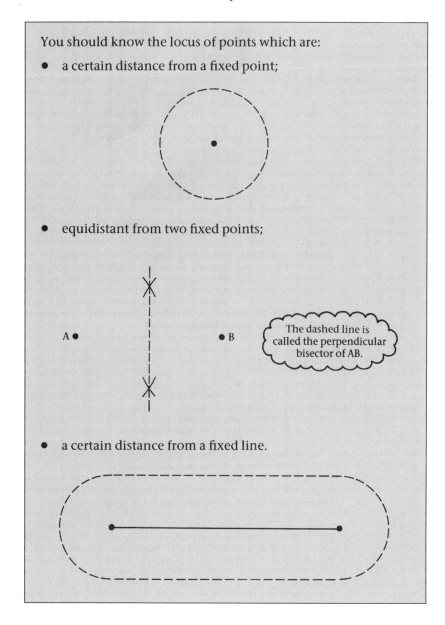

You should know the locus of points which are:

- a certain distance from a fixed point;

- equidistant from two fixed points;

A •         • B

The dashed line is called the perpendicular bisector of AB.

- a certain distance from a fixed line.

From these basic loci it is straightforward to shade in the regions of points which are:

- less or more than a certain distance from a fixed point;

- closer to one fixed point than another;

- less or more than a certain distance from a fixed line.

*EXERCISE 1*

**1** The diagram shows the plan view of a house in a garden.

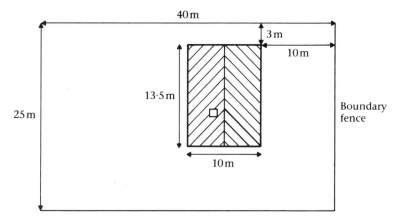

A tree is to be planted in the garden, but local regulations say that it must not be planted within 3 m of the boundary or within 4 m of the house. Draw a sketch of the garden and show as a shaded area the part of the garden where the tree can be planted.

**2** Mark a point P on a piece of paper. Shade the set of points which are more than 3 cm but less than 5 cm from P.

**3**

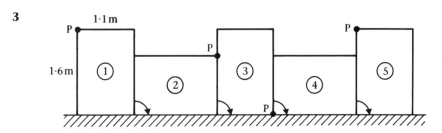

The diagram shows five different positions of a heavy packing case as it is moved in a straight line across a floor by turning it over and over. Draw the locus of the corner P, using a scale of 2 cm to 1 m.

**4** A and B are points 10 cm apart. Shade the locus of points which are nearer A than B and less than 7 cm from B.

**5** Suppose a bicycle is being ridden along a flat horizontal surface. Sketch the locus of:

(a) a point on the rim of a bicycle wheel;

(b) a point at the centre of a bicycle wheel.

## 1.2 Polygons

A **polygon** is the general name given to shapes such as triangles, quadrilaterals and hexagons which are made by joining straight lines together with no gaps. A triangle is a three-sided polygon and a quadrilateral is a four-sided polygon. A six-sided polygon, called a hexagon, is studied on tasksheet 2.

 TASKSHEET 2 – Orienteering (page 16)

At any corner of a polygon two angles are formed. The **interior angle** is the angle formed on the inside. On the tasksheet you saw that there was another important angle. This is the angle that you turn through at each corner as you trace round a polygon and is called the **exterior angle**.

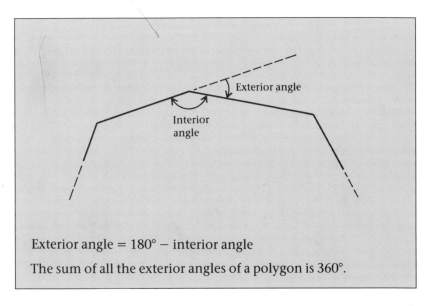

Exterior angle = 180° − interior angle

The sum of all the exterior angles of a polygon is 360°.

*EXAMPLE 3*

Find the sum of the interior angles of an octagon.

*SOLUTION*

An octagon has 8 sides and 8 corners. At each corner there is an interior angle and an exterior angle, the sum of the two angles being 180°.
So the sum of all interior and all exterior angles is $8 \times 180° = 1440°$.
The sum of the exterior angles is 360°.
So the sum of the interior angles must be $1440° - 360° = 1080°$.

(a) Use the method of example 3 to find the sums of the interior angles of polygons with 5, 6 and 7 sides. Then copy and complete the table.

| Name of polygon | Number of sides | Sum of angles (°) |
|---|---|---|
| Triangle | 3 | 180 |
| Quadrilateral | 4 | 360 |
| Pentagon | 5 | |
| Hexagon | 6 | |
| Heptagon | 7 | |
| Octagon | 8 | 1080 |

(b) Describe the pattern in the sequence of numbers in the last column.

(c) Extend the table to include the nonagon (9 sides) and the decagon (10 sides).

*EXERCISE 2*

**1**

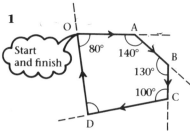

An orienteer runs around the course shown.

(a) Through what angle does he turn at A?

(b) When he reaches D, through what total angle has he turned from the start?

(c) Through what angle must he turn at D to return to the start point?

# 1.3 Regular polygons

The shape of a 50p coin is based on a regular seven-sided polygon (a regular heptagon). The curved sides of the coin are formed by an arc of the circle whose centre is the opposite corner.

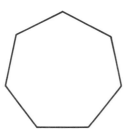  

In a regular polygon, all the sides are equal and all the angles are equal.

(a) Sketch a regular heptagon. (You can use a 50p coin to fix the corners and then use a ruler to join them.) On your sketch, draw in dashed lines to show the lines of symmetry.

(b) Write down the order of rotational symmetry. (The order of rotational symmetry is the number of times a shape fits onto its original position as it is rotated through 360°.)

(c) What name is given to a regular polygon with:

(i) 3 sides;   (ii) 4 sides?

(d) Describe the symmetry of these polygons.

*E X A M P L E 4*

Find the size of each angle of a regular heptagon.

*S O L U T I O N*

The word 'angle' without further qualification always means 'interior angle'.

You can find the answer from the basic idea that the sum of exterior angles is 360°.

Each of the equal exterior angles is $360° \div 7 = 51\frac{3}{7}°$ so each interior angle is $180° - 51\frac{3}{7}° = 128\frac{4}{7}°$.

11

For a regular polygon with $n$ sides:

- each exterior angle is $\dfrac{360°}{n}$ ;

- each interior angle is $180° - \dfrac{360°}{n}$ .

The diagram shows a **regular hexagon**.

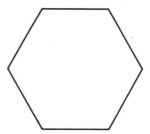

(a) On a sketch of a regular hexagon, draw in dashed lines to show the lines of symmetry and state the order of rotational symmetry.

(b) How many lines of symmetry has a regular polygon with $n$ sides?

(c) What can you say about the rotational symmetry of such a polygon?

(d) Draw hexagons which are **not** regular and yet have:

(i) equal sides; (ii) equal angles.

*TASKSHEET 3 — Regular tessellations (page 17)*

The only possible regular tessellations are of equilateral triangles, squares and hexagons.

A regular $n$-sided polygon has:

- $n$ lines of symmetry;

- rotational symmetry order $n$.

*EXERCISE 3*

**1** Find the exterior and interior angles of a regular decagon (ten-sided polygon).

**2** A regular octagon ABCDEFGH has centre O. Find the angles:

(a) AOB    (b) BAF

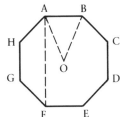

**3** A regular pentagon does not tessellate.

A pentagon such as the one illustrated does tessellate.

Show the tessellation on a sketch.

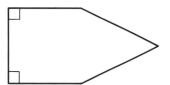

---

After working through this chapter you should:

1 know what is meant by a locus and be able to draw one;

2 understand what a polygon is;

3 know what the terms exterior angle and interior angle mean;

4 know which regular polygons tessellate and why;

5 be able to describe the symmetry of regular polygons;

6 be able to give a computer a set of instructions to draw a polygon.

# Two buoys

These questions are about the locus of a yacht moving in various directions relative to two marker buoys. As each locus takes some time to construct, it is a good idea for the class to be divided into four groups with each group looking at just one question thoroughly and reporting their findings to the whole class at the end. Discuss whether the locus has any symmetry and, if it does, try to explain why.

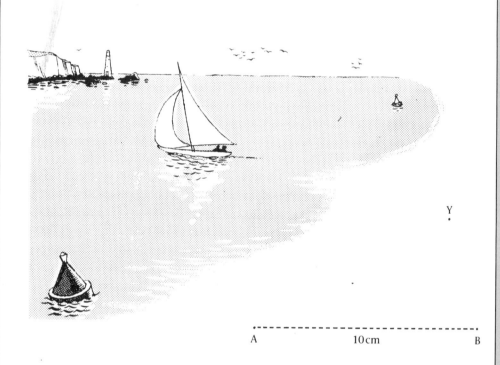

Y

A                    10cm                    B

The buoys are a kilometre apart. You can represent them as points A and B 10cm apart if you use a scale of 1cm to 100m. You can represent the yacht as a point Y.

**First locus**

The yacht sails so that the sum of its distances from the two buoys is 1·5 km.

Construction:

Mark A and B 10cm apart. Find a point $Y_1$ which is 10cm from A and 5cm from B. This represents a possible position of the yacht in your scale drawing. (You will find a pair of compasses useful.)

**1** Find several (at least ten) possible positions of the yacht and carefully draw the required locus.

### Second locus

The yacht sails so that the angle AYB is always 90°.

Construction:

Mark A and B 10cm apart. Lay a
set square with two edges passing
through A and B, as shown. Then the
point $Y_1$ is one possible position
of the yacht in your scale drawing.

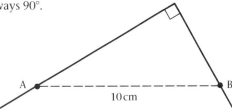

2    Find at least ten possible positions of the yacht on your scale drawing and carefully
draw the required locus.

### Third locus

The yacht sails so that its distance from A is always equal to its distance from B.

Construction:

Mark A and B 10cm apart. Set your compasses to a radius greater than 5cm and draw an
arc first from A then from B. (The arcs should intersect at two points.) They represent
two possible positions for the yacht.

3    Repeat this for several different lengths of radius (at least ten) and carefully draw the
required locus. Explain why you think the locus is called the **perpendicular
bisector** of AB.

### Fourth locus

The yacht sails so that its distance from A is always twice its distance from B.

Construction:

Mark A and B 10cm apart. Set your compasses to, for example, 4cm and draw an arc
from B. Double the radius (8cm if you used 4cm to start with) and draw an arc from A.
The arcs cross at two points. These represent two possible positions for the yacht.

4    Repeat for several different values (at least ten) and carefully draw the required
locus.

# Orienteering

In the sport of orienteering you run around a course following a route on a map. There are numbers on the map which refer to numbered posts which are placed at various points on the route. Each post also has a letter attached to it which is not given on the map. As you run around you record the letter against the number to prove that you have completed the route without cutting corners.

One of the routes at the Brandon Park Permanent Orienteering Course near Thetford Forest looks like this:

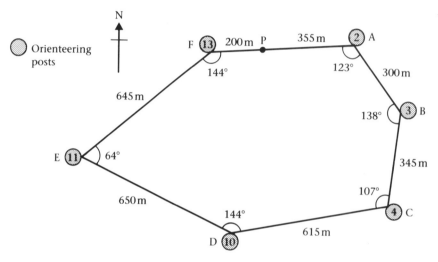

1  Use the computer programming language *LOGO* to draw the course on a computer screen. Start and finish at the point labelled P and go around the course in a clockwise direction.

2  As you go around the course you have to turn in a clockwise direction at each of the six points A, B, . . ., F.

   (a) What connection is there between the interior angle at A, 123°, and the angle you have to turn through?

   (b) Write down the angle you turn through at each corner. Show that the angles of turn add up to 360°.

3  Repeat questions 1 and 2 but go around the route in an anticlockwise direction.

4  A short circuit, again starting and finishing at P, passes through A, B, C and F and a medium circuit passes through A, B, D, E and F. Give a reason why the sum of the angles of turn (these are usually called **exterior** angles) will still be 360° for each circuit.

# Regular tessellations

Shapes that fit together like tiles on a floor or wall (without leaving gaps) are said to **tessellate**.

A regular tessellation is a tiling of a flat surface by identical shapes, each of which is a regular polygon.

**1**

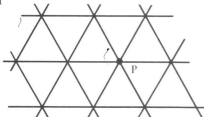

At a point P in a tessellation of equilateral triangles, six angles meet.

   (a)  What is the size of each angle?

   (b)  Explain why equilateral triangles of equal size tessellate.

**2**

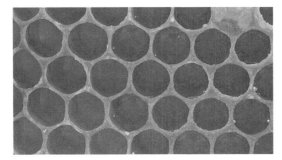
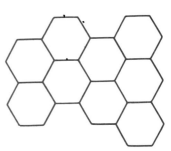

Calculate the size of the interior angle of a regular hexagon. Hence explain why regular hexagons tessellate.

**3**  Explain why regular pentagons do not tessellate.

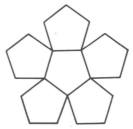

**4**  Two regular tessellations have been mentioned. The square is the only other regular polygon which tessellates. By considering the sizes of the angles of regular polygons with more than six sides, explain why there are no more regular tessellations.

# 2 Directions

## 2.1 Bearings

A school raises money by organising a raffle for a ride in a hot-air balloon. The balloon can carry four passengers. The direction in which it flies depends on the wind. On the day of the flight, the wind is blowing approximately from the south-west.

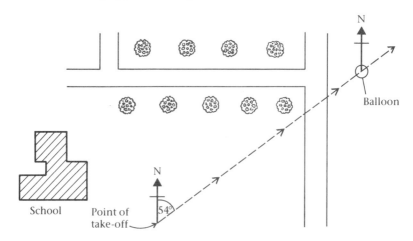

A spectator stands at the point of take-off and faces north. He then turns in a clockwise direction and faces the direction in which the balloon is heading. If the angle he turns through is 54°, then the balloon is said to be heading on a **bearing** of 054°.

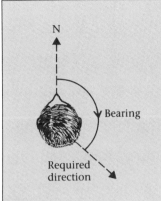

A bearing is the angle turned in a clockwise direction from north to the required direction.

Bearings are usually written using three figures to avoid possible error, so can take any value from 000° to 360°.

---

A passenger in the balloon looks back to the point of take-off and uses a compass to take a bearing.

What bearing does her compass show?

---

(a) Express the eight main compass points as three-figure bearings.

You will need a copy of datasheet 1 for the following questions.

(b) Give the bearing of a walker at grid reference (abbreviated to GR) 140866 from the triangulation point at GR 129878.

(c) Give the reverse bearing, that is the bearing of the triangulation point from the walker.

(d) Which feature lies 2·2 km on a bearing of 349° from Mam Tor at GR 127836?

(e) Find the distance and bearing of:

   (i) the cairn on Grindslow Knoll at GR 110868 from Mam Tor;

   (ii) Hollins Cross at GR 136845 from Grindslow Knoll cairn.

(f) Identify the feature 2·4 km from Hollins Cross on a bearing of 273°.

## 2.2 Fixing a position

Suppose that you are making a survey and want to fix the position of a tower on your map. Taking bearings on it, using a compass, is easy; but you don't know how far away it is. Suppose you take bearings on the tower from two different points which are already marked on the map.

> How can you fix the position of the tower?

*TASKSHEET 1 — Using two bearings (page 27)*

The Ordnance Survey Department uses bearings from two or more known positions when they need to fix the location of a geographical feature. You may have seen some of these known positions, commonly called **trig points**, which are often found near the tops of hills.

The procedure is called **triangulation**.

Triangulation is the method used in surveying to fix the positions of inaccessible features by taking bearings from two points, called trig points, whose positions are known accurately.

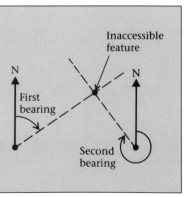

EXERCISE 1

**1** You will need datasheet 1 for this question.

Observers are stationed at the trig points at GR 128836 (Mam Tor) and GR 129878. They both take bearings on the same feature. From Mam Tor its bearing is 320° and from the other observation point its bearing is 203°. What is the feature?

**2**

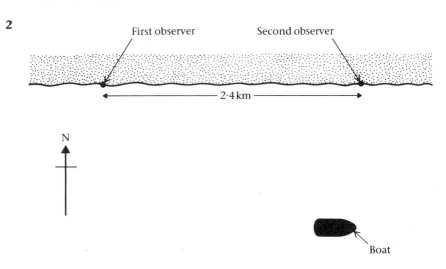

A boat sends out a distress signal. Two coastguard officers are standing at a distance of 2·4 km from each other on a coastline which runs directly east–west. At the same instant they each take bearings on the boat. The bearings taken by the two observers are 148° and 188° respectively. Find by scale drawing how far the boat is from the shore.

**3** A ship leaves harbour and sails at 24 km h⁻¹. It steers for three hours on a bearing of 124° and then for two hours on a bearing of 212°. Find by scale drawing:

(a) how far east and how far south it has travelled;

(b) its final distance and bearing from the harbour.

## 2.3 Vectors

You have seen how a journey can be described by its distance and direction given as a three-figure bearing. An alternative method uses a grid to define a journey.

Suppose that a hot-air balloon travels from GR 191853 to GR 196856.

The notation $\overrightarrow{AB}$ is used to represent the journey A to B.

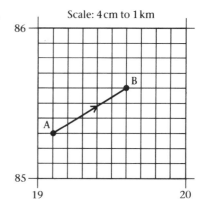

Scale: 4 cm to 1 km

Describe this journey using a distance and a bearing.

The journey can be described as '5 grid squares along and 3 grid squares up'. In mathematics, a **column vector** is used to denote a journey. A column vector is a column of numbers enclosed by square brackets. In this case:

$$\overrightarrow{AB} = \begin{bmatrix} 5 \\ 3 \end{bmatrix}$$

It might be more sensible to describe the journey in terms of distances on the ground rather than grid squares, in which case the journey is '0·5 km east and 0·3 km north'.

$$\overrightarrow{AB} = \begin{bmatrix} 0\cdot5 \\ 0\cdot3 \end{bmatrix} km$$

Journeys to the west and south are given **negative** numbers.

So, for example, the journey from B to A is $\overrightarrow{BA} = \begin{bmatrix} ^-0\cdot5 \\ ^-0\cdot3 \end{bmatrix} km$.

If M is at GR 192858 and N is at GR 197851 write the vector $\overrightarrow{MN}$ in terms of distance along the ground.

Vectors are also used in geometry to describe movement on an $x$–$y$ grid.

EXAMPLE 1

If P is (5, 1) and Q is (2, 6), write down the vector $\overrightarrow{PQ}$ as a column vector.

SOLUTION

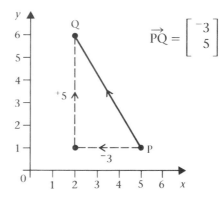

$$\overrightarrow{PQ} = \begin{bmatrix} ^-3 \\ 5 \end{bmatrix}$$

The vector $\overrightarrow{AB}$ denotes the journey from point A to point B.

$$\overrightarrow{AB} = \begin{bmatrix} \text{change in } x\text{-coordinate} \\ \text{change in } y\text{-coordinate} \end{bmatrix}$$

Changes are either positive or negative.

Changes in $x$:

- from left to right (or eastward) are positive;

- from right to left (or westward) are negative.

Changes in $y$:

- which go up the grid (or northward) are positive;

- which go down the grid (or southward) are negative.

In example 1, write down the vector $\overrightarrow{QP}$.

If a shape is moved to another part of the grid without rotation or reflection, then the movement is called a **translation** and is defined by a column vector.

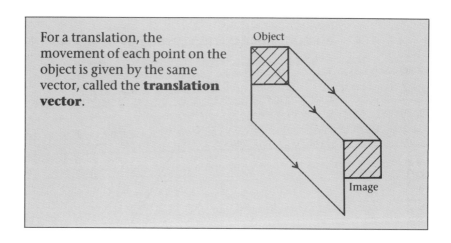

For a translation, the movement of each point on the object is given by the same vector, called the **translation vector**.

Object

Image

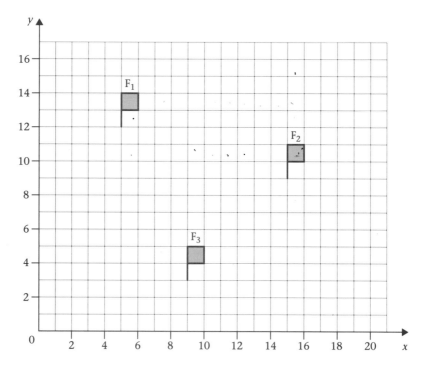

Write down the translation vector which sends the flag from:

(a) $F_1$ to $F_2$     (b) $F_2$ to $F_1$     (c) $F_1$ to $F_3$

(d) $F_3$ to $F_1$     (e) $F_2$ to $F_3$     (f) $F_3$ to $F_2$

## 2.4 Three dimensions

One of the attractions at a school's open day is the opportunity to experience a tethered flight in a hot-air balloon.

A spectator describes the position of the tethered balloon as follows:

Start at the take-off point and walk 30 metres due east. Then turn and walk 40 metres due north. The balloon is 50 metres directly above you.

The spectator has specified a position using the three numbers 30, 40 and 50. In two dimensions (in the plane), a point is given by two coordinates. In three dimensions (in space), a point needs three coordinates.

On the three-dimensional $(x, y, z)$ grid, B is the point $(30, 40, 50)$.

Sketching a box (shown with dashed lines) helps to create a three-dimensional picture.

In this case, the $y$- and $z$-axes are in the plane of the page, and you should think of the $x$-axis as coming out of the page towards you.

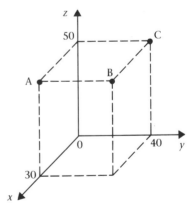

> Write down the coordinates of:
>
> (a) the mid-point of AB;
>
> (b) the mid-point of OC.

Axes can be shown in many different ways.
For example, these diagrams illustrate the same set of axes from
different points of views.

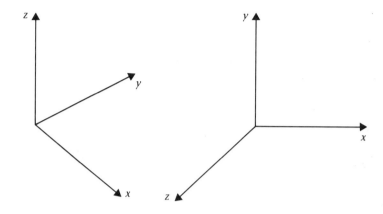

Copy both of the sets of axes illustrated and on each one show
the point (30, 40, 50) using a dashed cuboid as on the previous
page.

After working through this chapter you should:

1   be able to use distance and bearing to define a journey;

2   know how to use triangulation to fix a position;

3   know what a column vector is and how to use it to describe a
translation;

4   be able to describe a position in three dimensions using $(x, y, z)$
coordinates.

# Using two bearings

You will need datasheet 1.

You can determine the position of a feature by taking bearings on it from two points whose positions are accurately known.

A walker in the Peak District of Derbyshire is at the top of Back Tor (grid reference 145850) when she notices a crashed hang glider at the other side of the Edale Valley. She takes a bearing on the crash with her compass and finds that it is 321°.

**1** Mark the line on the datasheet along which the crash must lie.

The walker continues along the ridge to Hollins Cross (grid reference 136845) and takes another bearing on the crash. This time it is 351°.

**2** Mark a second line on which the crash must lie.

The walker now hurries to the village of Edale and reports the grid reference of the crash.

**3** What is the grid reference of the crash?

**4** How far, as the crow flies, is the crash from the National Park Information Centre (GR 126858)?

# 3 Right-angled triangles

## 3.1 Pythagoras' rule

Pythagoras was a Greek mathematician who lived from about 580 BC to about 500 BC. He is credited with an important discovery about triangles.

Pythagoras discovered that if you construct squares on each of the three sides of a triangle, then there is an interesting relationship between the areas of the three squares.

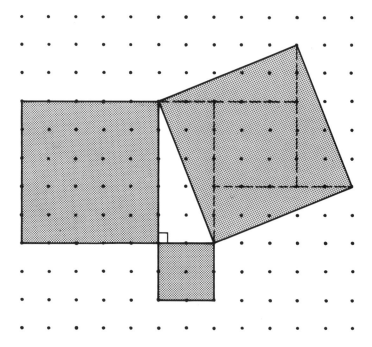

You can calculate the areas of the squares drawn on the triangle without measuring the sides with a ruler.

The two smaller squares have areas 4 and 25 square units.

The area of the large square can be calculated by dividing up the square as shown by the dashed lines.

> Show how this dissection enables you to calculate the area of the large square.

You may have noticed an interesting connection between the areas of the squares. However, the evidence of one triangle is not enough and you should look at several triangles before you make any rules.

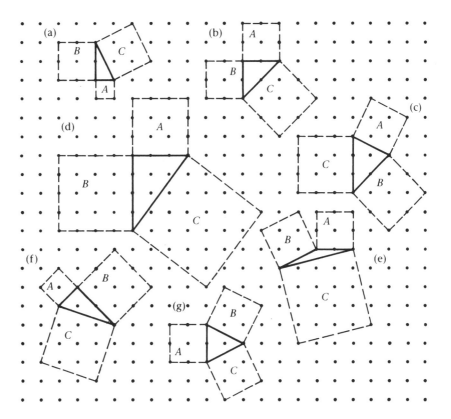

(a)  Calculate the areas of the squares drawn on the sides of each triangle. Use dissection where necessary. (You may find it helpful to copy these squares onto square dotted paper so that you can draw the dissection.)

(b)  In each case compare the area $A + B$ with area $C$. Describe what you find and discuss any rules you think might apply.

The rule you have discovered is called **Pythagoras' rule**. (You will find that many textbooks call the rule Pythagoras' theorem.)

You may feel that the evidence of half a dozen examples is still not very convincing. The tasksheet will provide you with a proof of the rule.

*TASKSHEET 1  —  Proving Pythagoras (page 38)*

The longest side of a right-angled triangle (the side opposite the right angle) is called the **hypotenuse**.

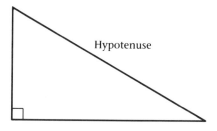

Pythagoras' rule states that for a right-angled triangle, the area of the square on the hypotenuse is equal to the sum of the areas of the squares on the other two sides.

Pythagoras' rule for right-angled triangles states that:

$$c^2 = a^2 + b^2$$

When you use Pythagoras' rule, always start by identifying the hypotenuse.

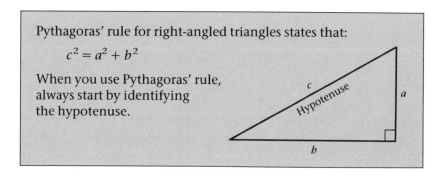

EXAMPLE 1

Use Pythagoras' rule to calculate $x$ (where all dimensions are in centimetres).

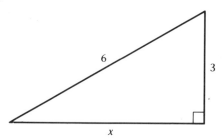

SOLUTION

The hypotenuse is 6 cm so $6^2 = x^2 + 3^2$

$$36 = x^2 + 9$$
$$x^2 = 27$$
$$x = \sqrt{27}$$
$$= 5\cdot20 \text{ cm} \quad \text{(to 2 d.p.)}$$

EXERCISE 1

**1** For each diagram use Pythagoras' rule to calculate the area marked *A*.

(a)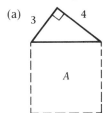

(b)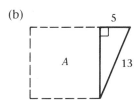

(c)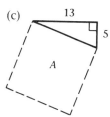

**2** (a) You can use Pythagoras' rule to calculate the missing length for two of these triangles. For which triangle can you **not** use the rule? (Explain why not.)

(i)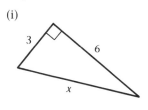

(ii)

(iii)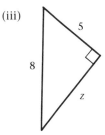

(b) For the two triangles where it is appropriate to use Pythagoras' rule, calculate the missing lengths.

**3** Use Pythagoras' rule to calculate the lengths of these lines by making each into the hypotenuse of a right-angled triangle as shown in (a).

(a)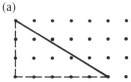

(b)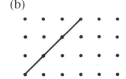

(c)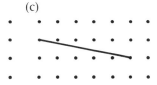

**4** Four identical guy-ropes are used to secure a flag pole as illustrated, where all dimensions are in centimetres. Calculate the length of each rope.

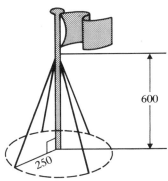

600

250

## 3.2 Pythagorean triples

The right angle is an important feature in architecture and the ability to construct accurate right angles has always been an essential requirement in the building trade. The pyramids would have looked much less impressive if the builders had been unable to construct accurate right angles! Indeed, there is evidence that many ancient civilisations were familiar with the results of Pythagoras' rule and that they used these results in building and surveying.

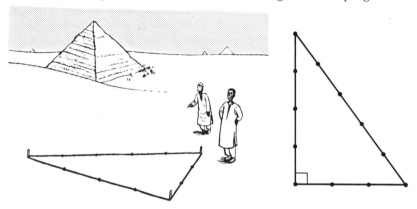

The 3 : 4 : 5 triangle illustrated shows the best known **Pythagorean triple**. A Pythagorean triple is a set of three whole numbers which could represent the lengths of the sides of a right-angled triangle.

(a) How do you know that a triangle with sides of length 3, 4 and 5 must be a right-angled triangle?

The following table shows some Pythagorean triples.

| $a$ | $b$ | $c$ |
|-----|-----|-----|
| 3 | 4 | 5 |
| 5 | 12 | 13 |
| 7 | 24 | 25 |

(b) Use Pythagoras' rule to check the values given in the table.

(c) Find at least one other Pythagorean triple.

  T A S K S H E E T  2  —  *Similar triangles (page 39)*

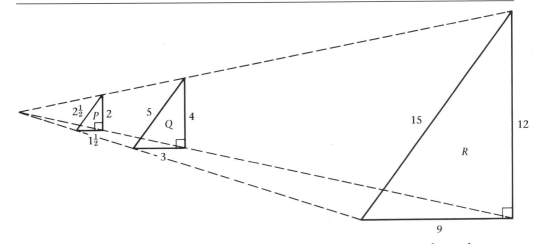

These triangles are all **similar**. That is, any one triangle can be considered as a simple enlargement of any other.

> Calculate the enlargement scale factor used to transform:
>
> (a)  triangle $Q$ to triangle $R$;
>
> (b)  triangle $Q$ to triangle $P$;
>
> (c)  triangle $P$ to triangle $R$.

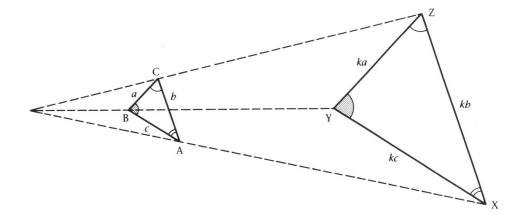

For any two similar triangles:

- corresponding angles are equal;

- corresponding sides are in the same ratio. That is:

$$\frac{YZ}{BC} = \frac{XZ}{AC} = \frac{XY}{AB} = k$$

where $k$ is the scale factor of enlargement.

## 3.3 The tangent of an angle

A student stands 8 m from the base of the sheer cliff face of a climbing wall at a sports centre. She uses a clinometer to measure the angle of elevation of her friend.

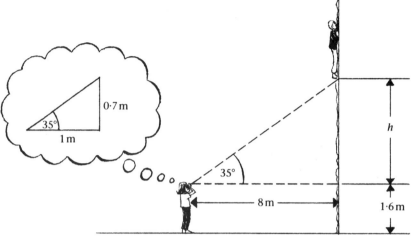

From previous experience, she knows that for a 35° angle, you go up 0·7 m for every 1 m you go along.

So for 8 m along, you go up $8 \times 0\cdot7 = 5\cdot6$ m.

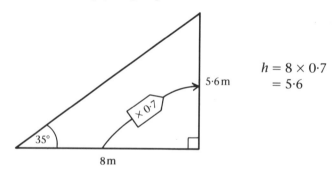

$$h = 8 \times 0\cdot7$$
$$= 5\cdot6$$

Her friend is $1\cdot6 + 5\cdot6 = 7\cdot2$ metres above ground level.

Accurately construct a 35° right-angled triangle of your own choice and show that, whatever size triangle you choose, it is always true that $a \times 0\cdot7 = b$.

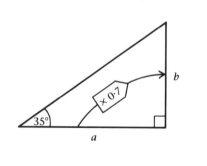

You have seen that 0·7 is a special multiplier associated with the angle 35°. This multiplier is given the name **tan** 35°, which is short for the **tangent** of 35°. The size of the multiplier depends on the size of the angle. The table shows the multiplier for different angles.

| Angle θ | Multiplier tan θ |
|---------|------------------|
| 10° | 0·176 |
| 20° | 0·364 |
| 30° | 0·577 |
| **35°** | **0·700** |
| 40° | 0·839 |
| 50° | 1·192 |
| 60° | 1·732 |
| 70° | 2·747 |
| 80° | 5·671 |

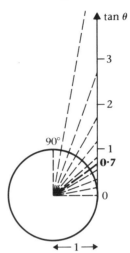

Greek letters such as θ (theta) are often used for the size of angles.

The reason why the word tangent is used can be seen from the diagram where the line showing the multipliers is a tangent to the circle showing the angles.

(a) For what angle θ does tan θ = 1?

(b) What is the value of tan 0°?

(c) Why is tan 90° not shown in the table?

In a right-angled triangle, to calculate the side opposite the angle θ you multiply the side adjacent to θ by tan θ.

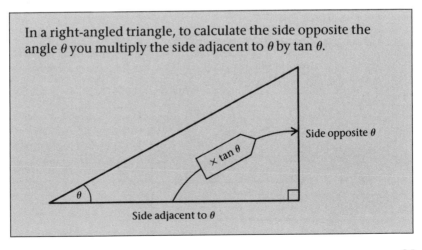

35

## EXAMPLE 2

Calculate the height of the tree shown in this picture.

## SOLUTION

Since you are asked to 'calculate' the height of the tree you should **not** use a scale drawing to solve the problem. However, you can use the information from the table on the previous page.

Always include a sketch of the triangle in your solution when answering this type of question.

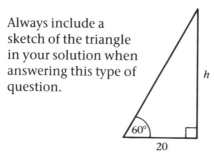

$h = 20 \times \tan 60°$
$= 20 \times 1·732$
$= 34·64$

So the tree is about 35 m tall.

## EXERCISE 2

**1** For each of these triangles, calculate the length opposite the angle.

(a)

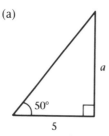

(b)

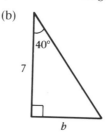

(c)

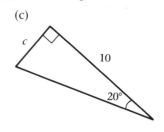

**2** For each of these triangles, calculate the unknown length denoted by a letter. (Remember to use the angle which is adjacent to the length you know.)

(a)

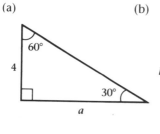

(b)

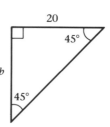

(c)

**3**  For each of these triangles, calculate the value of tan $\theta$ and hence estimate the value of $\theta$ from the table given on page 35.

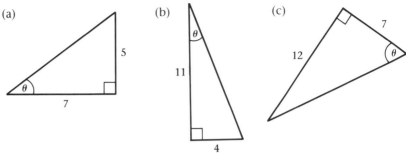

(a)

(b)

(c)

**4**  A window cleaner's ladder makes an angle of 20° with a wall when it just reaches a window 5 metres up. How far is the foot of the ladder from the building? (First draw a diagram to illustrate the problem.)

After working through this chapter you should:

1  know Pythagoras' rule for right-angled triangles and how to use it to solve problems;

2  know what similar triangles are;

3  know what an enlargement is and how to calculate a scale factor of enlargement;

4  know what the tangent of an angle (tan $\theta$) means, and how to use it to solve problems.

# Proving Pythagoras

1 (a) For the right-angled triangle shown below, draw 4 copies onto squared paper and also one copy of the square shown:

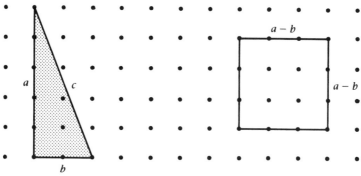

(b) Cut out the shapes and fit them together to form a large square.

(c) Fit the shapes together to form two squares as shown.

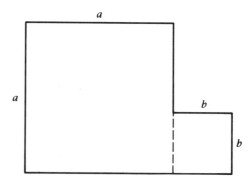

(d) Explain how this shows that $a^2 + b^2 = c^2$.

2 Repeat for any right-angled triangle of your own choosing.

# Similar triangles

Throughout the ages, builders have constructed right angles using a length of rope with twelve equally-spaced knots. This is then pegged out to form a 3 : 4 : 5 triangle.

It does not matter what length of rope you have to start with. A small length simply gives a small triangle.

**1**   (a)   Construct these triangles on a sheet of square dotted paper.

   (i)   a 3 : 4 : 5 triangle

   (ii)   a 6 : 8 : 10 triangle

   (iii)   a 9 : 12 : 15 triangle

   (b)   Carefully describe what is **similar** about the three triangles.

**2**   An enlargement of a triangle ABC with scale factor 2 and centre O is illustrated.

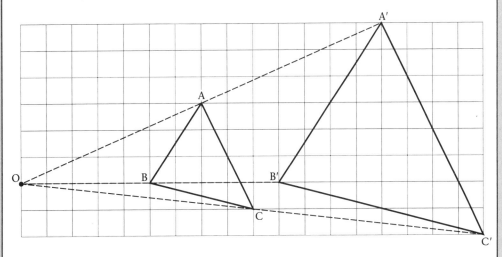

Copy the diagram onto centimetre-square dotted paper.

(a) Take measurements from the diagram and compare the angles:

   (i) ABC and A′B′C′    (ii) BAC and B′A′C′

   What do you notice?

(b) Use Pythagoras' rule to calculate the lengths:

   (i) OA and OA′    (ii) AB and A′B′

   (iii) BC and B′C′    (iv) CA and C′A′

   Check your calculations by measuring the lengths and calculate again any that are clearly wrong.

   What do you notice about the pairs of lengths?

(c) Use the lengths calculated in (b) to evaluate:

   (i) AB ÷ AC and A′B′ ÷ A′C′

   (ii) AB ÷ BC and A′B′ ÷ B′C′

   What do you notice?

**3**  The diagram shows an enlargement of the triangle ABC with scale factor $\frac{1}{2}$, centre O. (Using a scale factor less than 1 results in a reduction in size.)

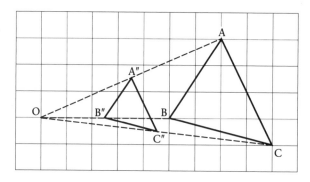

In what way are the two triangles similar?

# 4 Perimeters and areas

## 4.1 Circumference of a circle

This chapter investigates the properties of different shapes and you will also be calculating their perimeters and areas. In particular, you will consider circles, parallelograms and trapeziums.

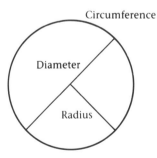

As you have seen in chapter 1, a circle is the locus of points which are all the same distance from a central point. The distance around the circle, its perimeter, is usually called its **circumference**.

TASKSHEET 1 — *Circumference of a circle (page 54)*

---

The formula for the circumference, $C$, of a circle of radius $r$ is:

$$C = 2\pi r \quad \text{or} \quad C = \pi d$$

where $\pi = 3 \cdot 14159 \ldots$ and $d = $ diameter $= 2r$.

---

When calculating, you can use the $\pi$ button on your calculator. Before the days of calculators, the fraction $\frac{22}{7}$ was often used as an approximation to $\pi$.

You can sometimes use 3 as a rough approximation to $\pi$ when you want to do quick calculations in your head.

(a) How accurate is the approximation $\pi \approx \frac{22}{7}$ ?

(b) For each of these circles, calculate the circumference, first by doing a mental calculation using $\pi \approx 3$, and then by using your calculator to obtain an accurate solution.

(i)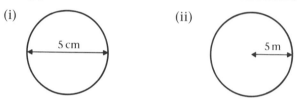

5 cm

(ii)

5 m

*EXAMPLE 1*

A forester is working with a chain saw with a blade of length 45 cm. He uses a tape to measure the girth (circumference) of a tree and finds it to be 250 cm. Will he be able to fell the tree using the chain saw?

## SOLUTION

With care, it is just possible to cut down a tree if the blade will reach the centre. Taking the cross-section of the tree to be a circle and the length of the blade to be the radius, the forester can use the formula $C = 2\pi r$ to see if he can cut down the tree.

$$2 \times 3 \times 45 = 270\,\text{cm}$$

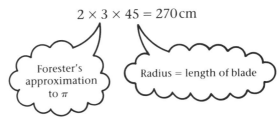

Forester's approximation to $\pi$

Radius = length of blade

Since the actual girth (250 cm) is less than 270 cm, the forester should be able to fell the tree. In practice he would use a larger chain saw if one were available.

### EXERCISE 1

1   To answer this question use any circular coins you have. For at least two coins:

   • measure the diameter;

   • calculate the circumference;

   • measure the distance a coin travels when you roll it through one turn.

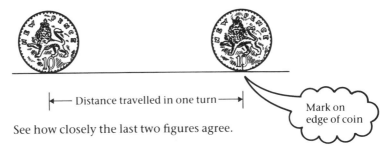

← Distance travelled in one turn →

Mark on edge of coin

See how closely the last two figures agree.

2   A circle has a circumference of 18 cm.

   (a) Use the rough estimate $\pi \approx 3$ to find an approximation to its diameter.

   (b) Use your calculator to find the diameter correct to 2 decimal places.

3   A joiner has cut out a circular table top with radius 80 cm and wants to edge it with a stick-on strip. What length of strip will she need?

4   A bicycle wheel has a diameter of 70 cm.

   (a) How far does it travel in one turn?

   (b) How many turns does it make in a journey of 2 km?

## 4.2 Area of a circle

A circle of radius $r$ has a square outside and another square inside, as shown.

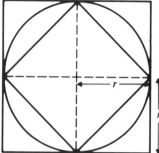

Explain why the area of the circle is:

- smaller than $4r^2$;

- larger than $2r^2$.

As you might expect, the number $\pi$ occurs in the exact formula for the area.

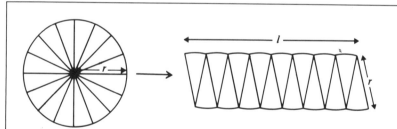

A circle is cut up into many equal sectors which are then fitted together as shown.

(a) Describe the shape on the right.

(b) What happens as the number of sectors is increased?

(c) What is the value of $l$ in terms of $r$?

(d) What is the area of the circle?

The formula for the area of a circle of radius $r$ is:

$$A = \pi r^2$$

*EXAMPLE 2*

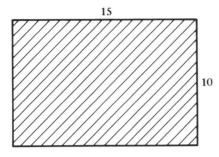

Find the area of the largest circle which can be cut from this rectangular sheet of card. (Dimensions are in cm.)

*SOLUTION*

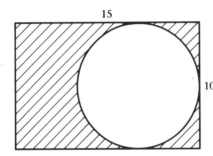

The circle shown is the largest.

Diameter = 10 cm
Radius    = 5 cm
Area      $= \pi \times 5^2$
          $= \pi \times 25$
          $= 78 \cdot 5 \, \text{cm}^2$ (to 1 d.p.)

How much card would be wasted?

You may be given the area of a circle and have to find its radius.

*EXAMPLE 3*

A researcher in optics wants to make a disc of area $10 \, \text{cm}^2$. What radius should she use?

*SOLUTION*

If the radius is $r$ cm:

$$\pi r^2 = 10$$
$$r^2 = 10 \div \pi \approx 3 \cdot 183$$
$$r = \sqrt{3 \cdot 183} = 1 \cdot 78 \quad \text{(to 2 d.p.)}$$

She should use a radius of $1 \cdot 78$ cm.

EXERCISE 2

**1**   Calculate the circumferences and areas of these circles. (Dimensions are in cm.)

(a) 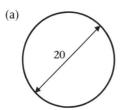   (b) 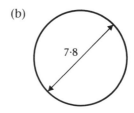   (c)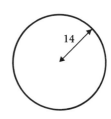

**2**   Calculate the perimeters and areas of these shapes. (Dimensions are in cm.)

(a) 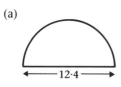   (b)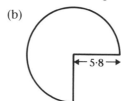

**3**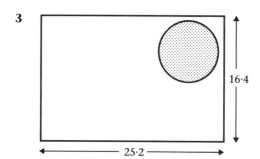

Discs of radius 4 cm are stamped out of a sheet of metal of area 25·2 cm × 16·4 cm.

(a) How many discs can be stamped from the sheet?

(b) What area of the sheet is wasted?

**4**   The area of a circle is 12 cm².

(a) Use the rough estimate $\pi \approx 3$ to find its radius approximately.

(b) Use your calculator to find the radius correct to 2 decimal places.

**5E**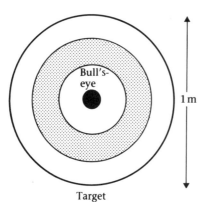

An archery target has a diameter of 1 m. The area of the bull's-eye is one hundredth of the total area of the target. What is the diameter of the bull's-eye?

## 4.3 The parallelogram

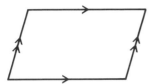

A parallelogram is a quadrilateral with two pairs of parallel sides.

Describe the symmetry properties of a parallelogram.

*TASKSHEET 2 — Area of a parallelogram (page 55)*

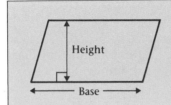

The formula for the area of a parallelogram is:

area = base × height

### EXAMPLE 4

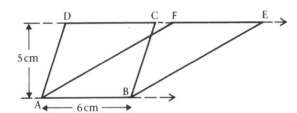

AB and DE are parallel lines 5 cm apart.
AB = 6 cm
ABCD and ABEF are parallelograms. Find their areas.

### SOLUTION

Both parallelograms have base of length 6 cm and height of length 5 cm and so each parallelogram has area $6 \times 5 = 30\,cm^2$.

All parallelograms on the same base and between the same parallel lines have the same area.

Although the word 'base' is used in the formula for the area of a parallelogram it does not always mean the bottom of the figure.

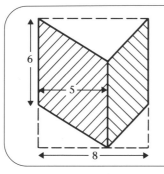

The total shaded area consists of two parallelograms 'back to back'. (Dimensions are in cm.) Find the area.

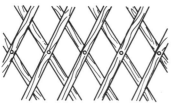

A particularly important parallelogram is one whose sides are all equal so that it is shaped like the diamond on a playing card. This diamond shape is called a **rhombus**.

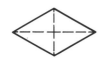

Describe how the diagonals of a rhombus cross.

*EXERCISE 3*

**1** Find the areas of these shapes. (Dimensions are in cm.)

(a)

4·2

6·3

(b)

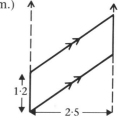

1·2

2·5

**2** Calculate the areas of these shapes. (Dimensions are in cm.)

(a)

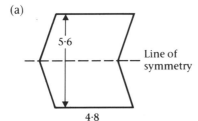

5·6

Line of symmetry

4·8

(b)

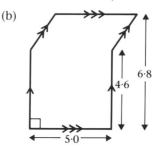

6·8

4·6

5·0

48

## 4.4 The trapezium

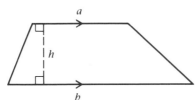

A **trapezium** is a quadrilateral with a pair of parallel sides.

Suppose two trapeziums, identical (congruent) to the one shown above, are put together to form a single quadrilateral as shown below.

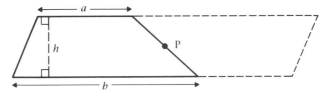

Each trapezium can be mapped onto the other by a 180° rotation about the point P.

(a) What type of quadrilateral is the combined shape?

(b) Explain why the area of each trapezium is $\frac{1}{2}(a + b)h$.

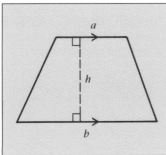

The formula for the area, $A$, of a trapezium is:

$$A = \tfrac{1}{2}(a + b) \times h$$

This can be thought of as the average of the parallel sides multiplied by the distance between them.

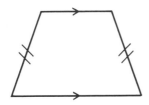

One particular trapezium shape is the **isosceles trapezium**, in which the two non-parallel sides are equal.

Sketch an isosceles trapezium, mark on its line of symmetry, and show clearly which angles are equal.

EXERCISE 4

1 Find the areas of these trapeziums. (Dimensions are in cm.)

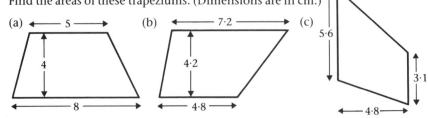

(a) 5, 4, 8

(b) 7·2, 4·2, 4·8

(c) 5·6, 3·1, 4·8

2 2·8 cm

Area = 9·2 cm²

4·9 cm

Find the distance between the parallel sides of this trapezium.

3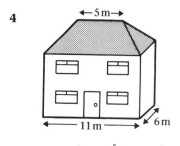

15, 7

An ornamental tile has the design shown. It is divided into a square and four congruent isosceles trapeziums.
Find the area of each trapezium. (Dimensions are in cm.)

4 ←5 m→

11 m, 6 m

The roof of this house is constructed from two isosceles triangles and two isosceles trapeziums as illustrated.

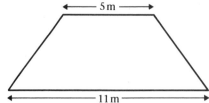

5 m, 11 m

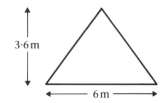

3·6 m, 6 m

A roofing contractor has to estimate the cost of replacing the slates on the roof. He charges £20 per square metre.

(a) Calculate the area of the roof.

(b) Calculate the cost of replacing the roof.

# 4.5 Classifying quadrilaterals

Quadrilaterals are classified into various types according to the properties of their sides and angles.

The diagram illustrates the main relationships between the important types of quadrilaterals.

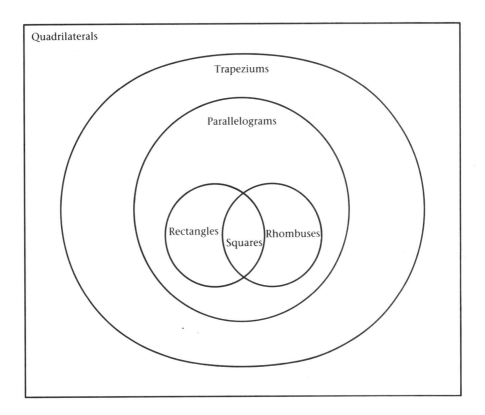

| | |
|---|---|
| Trapezium: | A quadrilateral with a pair of parallel sides. |
| Parallelogram: | A quadrilateral with two pairs of parallel sides. |
| Rhombus: | A parallelogram with all sides equal. |
| Rectangle: | A parallelogram with a right angle. |
| Square: | A rhombus with a right angle |
| | or |
| | a rectangle with all sides equal. |

Look at the diagram and answer these questions.

(a) Is a rectangle a parallelogram?

(b) Is a parallelogram a rectangle?

## 4.6 **Composite shapes**

Sometimes you can find the
area of a shape by dividing
it up into simpler shapes.

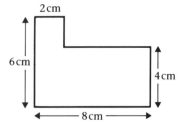

(a) Find the area of the shape illustrated by considering it to be
made from two simpler shapes.

(b) Find the area of the shape illustrated by considering it to be
a larger shape with a section removed.

*EXAMPLE 5*

The diagram shows the cross-section of a
copper tube. If the thickness of the metal
is 2 mm, find the shaded area.

*SOLUTION*

The shaded area is the difference between the area of the outer circle
and the area of the inner circle.

The radius of the outer circle is 0·9 cm so the area is
$\pi \times (0·9)^2 = 2·54$ cm$^2$ (to 2 d.p.).
The radius of the inner circle is 0·7 cm so the area is
$\pi \times (0·7)^2 = 1·54$ cm$^2$ (to 2 d.p.).
The shaded area is $(2·54 - 1·54)$ cm$^2 = 1·0$ cm$^2$.

A shaded area such as this is called a ring or an **annulus**.

*EXERCISE 5*

**1** Show that the area of each of the shapes below is 28 cm$^2$.

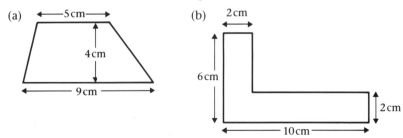

**2** 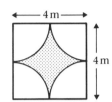 In a rifle target, the radii of the circles in centimetres are 1, 2, 3 and 4.

Find the areas of the bull's-eye and the three rings.

**3** Find the areas of these flower beds (shaded areas).

(a)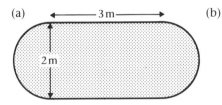

(b)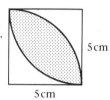

**4E** (a) Find the shaded area. (b) Use your answer to part (a) to show that this shaded area is approximately $14 \cdot 3 \, \text{cm}^2$.

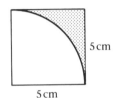

5 cm

5 cm

5 cm

5 cm

---

After working through this chapter you should:

1 understand and be able to apply the formulas for the circumference and area of a circle;

2 be able to find the areas of parallelograms and trapeziums;

3 be able to find the area of a composite shape by regarding it as being made up from simpler shapes;

4 be able to classify quadrilaterals such as:

- squares,

- rhombuses,

- rectangles,

- trapeziums,

- parallelograms,

- isosceles trapeziums.

# Circumference of a circle

> You will need a collection of circular objects of various sizes, a length of string, a ruler or tape measure and some graph paper.

1 For each object:

- measure its diameter as accurately as you can using the ruler or tape;
- measure its circumference, using the string by wrapping it round the object;
- collect your results together in a table like this.

| Object | Diameter, $d$ cm | Circumference, $C$ cm | $\dfrac{C}{d}$ |
|---|---|---|---|
| Plate | 14·3 | 45·2 | 3·2 |
| Bicycle wheel | . . . | . . . | . . . |
| . . . | . . . | . . . | . . . |

2 (a) What do you notice about the $\dfrac{C}{d}$ column?

(b) Do you think you need to check any measurements?

3 (a) Now plot circumference against diameter with axes as shown. Draw a straight line of best fit through the points.

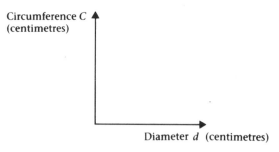

(b) What is the gradient of your line?

(c) How does the gradient compare with the values for $\dfrac{C}{d}$ given in the table?

(d) Does your line go through the origin?

(e) What is the equation of your line?

# Area of a parallelogram

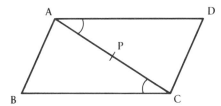

ABCD is a parallelogram.

You can see that triangles ABC and CDA are **congruent** because triangle ABC can be mapped onto triangle ACD by a 180° rotation about point P.

**1** Explain why the marked angles are equal.

**2** Which other angles are equal?

**3** By taking suitable measurements, calculate the area of triangle ABC.

**4** Use your answer to question 3 to calculate the area of parallelogram ABCD.

Another way to find the area of parallelogram ABCD is based on the idea of cutting along the line CM.

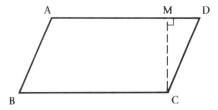

**5** Draw a diagram to show how the two parts of the parallelogram then fit together to make a rectangle.

**6** Check that the area of this rectangle is the same area as that found in question 4.

# 5 Three-dimensional shapes

## 5.1 Introduction

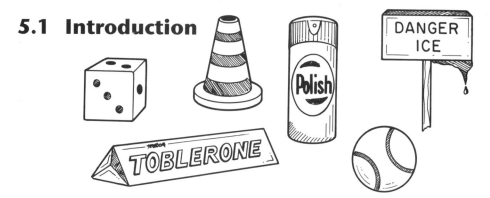

In this chapter you will learn how to work out the surface areas and volumes of three-dimensional shapes.

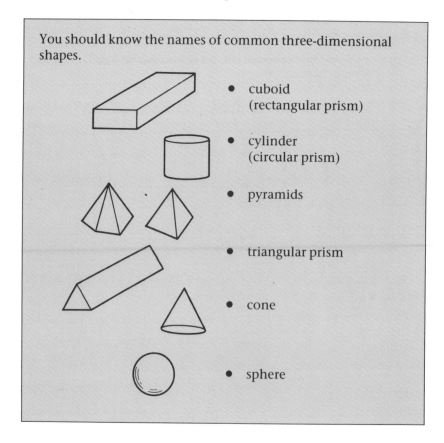

You should know the names of common three-dimensional shapes.

- cuboid
  (rectangular prism)

- cylinder
  (circular prism)

- pyramids

- triangular prism

- cone

- sphere

# 5.2 Prisms

EXAMPLE 1

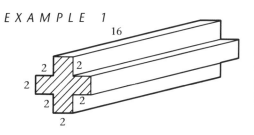

A metal component has dimensions (in centimetres) as shown. Find its volume.

SOLUTION

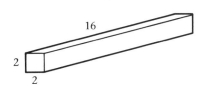

You can think of the solid as being made up of five rectangular blocks like this. Each block is 2 cm × 2 cm × 16 cm and so has volume 64 cm$^3$.
The total volume is:

$$5 \times 64 = 320 \text{ cm}^3$$

Another way of answering example 1 is to note that $(5 \times 2 \times 2)\,\text{cm}^2$ is the area of the end of the solid, shown shaded. Then the volume of the solid is the area of the end multiplied by the length, that is $(5 \times 2 \times 2) \times 16 = 320\,\text{cm}^3$.

The component in example 1 is a solid of uniform cross-section and is called a prism.

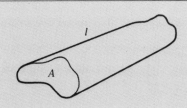

A prism is a solid which shows the same shape of section wherever it is cut at right angles to its length.

If the cross-section area is $A$ and the length is $l$ then the volume of the prism is $Al$.

(a)

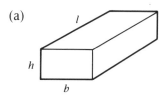

Explain why the formula for the volume of this cuboid, $V = lbh$, agrees with the formula $V = Al$, where $A$ is the area of cross-section.

(b) Explain why the volume of a cylinder with radius $r$ and height $h$ is $\pi r^2 h$.

### EXAMPLE 2

(a) Some copper tubing has an external diameter of 2·0 cm. The thickness of the copper is 2 mm. Calculate the area of cross-section of the tubing.

(b) If 1 cm$^3$ of copper weighs 7·8 g find the weight of a 4 m length of the tubing.

### SOLUTION

(a) The cross-section of the tubing is shown. Its area is:

$$(\pi \times 1\cdot0^2) - (\pi \times 0\cdot8^2) \approx 1\cdot13\,\text{cm}^2$$

(b) The volume of a 4-metre length is:

$$1\cdot13 \times 400 = 452\,\text{cm}^3$$

The weight of the copper tubing is:

$$452 \times 7\cdot8 \approx 3500\,\text{g}$$
$$\text{or} \quad 3\cdot5\,\text{kg} \quad \text{(to 1 d.p.)}$$

---

### EXERCISE 1

**1** Find the volume of a 20 cm × 15 cm tile with thickness 6 mm. (Take care with units!)

**2** Find the volume of a circular disc of diameter 6·4 cm and thickness 0·4 cm.

**3**

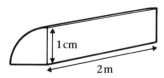

The moulding illustrated is a quadrant of a cylindrical piece of wood. Find its volume.

**4**

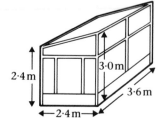

A gardener has a lean-to greenhouse with the dimensions shown. He wants to fumigate it by burning sulphur candles. The instructions on a candle say that it will fumigate a volume of 12 m$^3$.

How many candles should he burn?

## 5.3 Nets

A net is a two-dimensional shape which can be folded to make a three-dimensional shape.

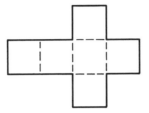

A well-known net is shown here. If the net is folded along the dotted lines then the edges will meet to form a hollow cube.

*EXAMPLE 3*

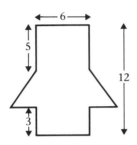

The shape shown, with dimensions in centimetres, is the net of a solid.

Sketch the solid and find its volume.

*SOLUTION*

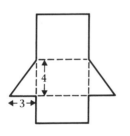

The fold-lines and two sides of a triangle are marked on the diagram. Because the triangle is right-angled its third side is 5 cm long, because $3^2 + 4^2 = 5^2$ (by Pythagoras' rule).

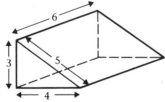

The solid produced by folding the net is a triangular prism.
The area of cross-section is:

$$\tfrac{1}{2}(3 \times 4) = 6\,\text{cm}^2$$

Using the formula $V = Al$, its volume is:

$$6 \times 6 = 36\,\text{cm}^3$$

(a) Calculate the area of the net.

(b) Sketch two other possible nets for the same triangular prism.

> The surface area of a solid shape is the area of its net.

*EXERCISE 2*

**1** Two nets are illustrated. Sketch and describe the three-dimensional shapes they make.

(a)

(b)

**2**

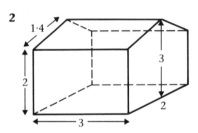

A shed has a floor $2\,\text{m} \times 3\,\text{m}$. Its height at the eaves is $2\,\text{m}$ and at the ridge $3\,\text{m}$.

(a) Draw a net for a model of the shed, including the floor, using a scale of $1\,\text{cm}$ to $1\,\text{m}$.

(b) Find the total surface area including the roof and the floor.

(c) Find the volume of air in the shed.

**3**

One face fits here.

The diagram shows the net of a solid with the two end-faces missing. You are shown where one of the faces should be.

(a) What is the shape of each of the missing end-faces?

(b) Where should the second missing end-face be?

**4E**

8 cm

$x$ cm

←10cm→

The shape illustrated is the net of a solid with a curved face.

(a) Sketch the solid.

(b) Find $x$.

(c) Find the volume of the solid.

(d) Find the surface area of the solid.

 *TASKSHEET 1E* — *Cube structures (page 63)*

## 5.4 Dimensions

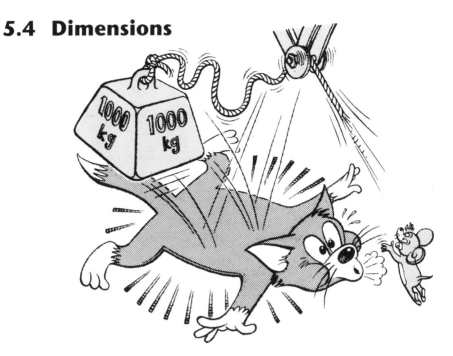

You have used formulas to calculate:

- lengths;
- areas;
- volumes.

Sometimes people use the wrong formula. A common mistake is to confuse the formulas $2\pi r$ and $\pi r^2$.

> What do these formulas stand for?

When you are in doubt, you can check what a formula is about by using the dimensions represented by the symbols. In a formula:

- numbers such as 2, 0·6, $\sqrt{2}$ and $\pi$ have **no dimensions**;
- letters such as $r$, $d$, $C$ and $l$ stand for **lengths**;
- when two lengths are multiplied, the result stands for an **area**;
- when three lengths are multiplied, the result stands for a **volume**.

> A student uses the formula $\frac{2}{3}\pi r^2$ for the volume of a hemisphere. Why must she be mistaken?

*EXAMPLE 4*

What does the formula $2\pi rh$ stand for?

*SOLUTION*

Start by analysing the dimensions.

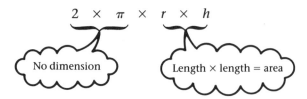

The formula represents length × length = area.

The use of $\pi$ and $r$ suggests a circle and $h$ suggests a cylinder. You might guess that the formula is for the curved surface area of a cylinder.

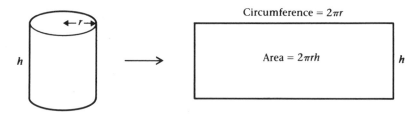

After working through this chapter you should:

1   know how to calculate volumes of prisms with simple cross-sections;

2   be able to draw nets of simple solids;

3   be able to draw simple solids, given their nets;

4   be able to work out whether a given formula represents a length, an area or a volume.

# Cube structures

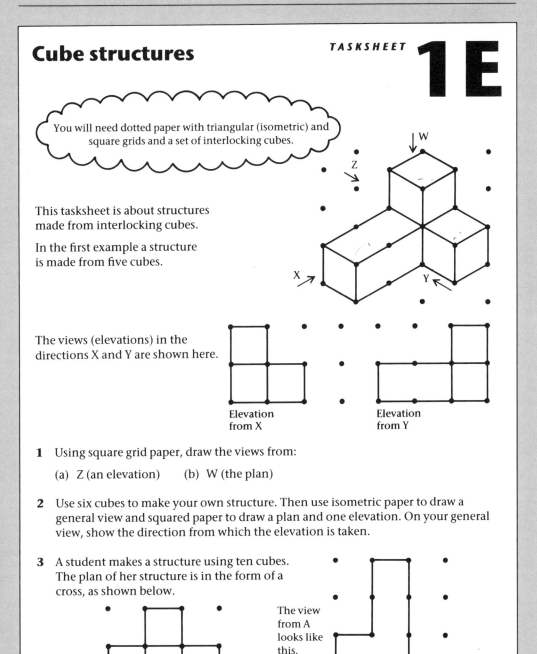

You will need dotted paper with triangular (isometric) and square grids and a set of interlocking cubes.

This tasksheet is about structures made from interlocking cubes.

In the first example a structure is made from five cubes.

The views (elevations) in the directions X and Y are shown here.

Elevation from X

Elevation from Y

**1** Using square grid paper, draw the views from:

(a) Z (an elevation)   (b) W (the plan)

**2** Use six cubes to make your own structure. Then use isometric paper to draw a general view and squared paper to draw a plan and one elevation. On your general view, show the direction from which the elevation is taken.

**3** A student makes a structure using ten cubes. The plan of her structure is in the form of a cross, as shown below.

The view from A looks like this.

Elevation from A

Use ten cubes to make a structure with this plan and elevation. Then on square paper draw the views (elevations) from B and from C.

# 6 Trigonometry

## 6.1 Using a calculator

In chapter 3 you used these values for tan $\theta$.

| $\theta$ | tan $\theta$ |
|---|---|
| 10° | 0·176 |
| 20° | 0·364 |
| 30° | 0·577 |
| 35° | 0·700 |
| 40° | 0·839 |
| 50° | 1·192 |
| 60° | 1·732 |
| 70° | 2·747 |
| 80° | 5·671 |

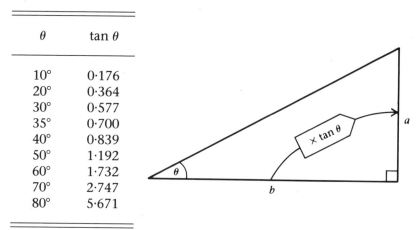

You can use a scientific calculator to obtain more accurate values of tan $\theta$ for these and other angles. First check that your calculator is in degree mode. (Angles can be measured in other units called radians and grads. You should always work in degrees.)

To obtain an accurate value of, for example, tan 35°, you type in 35 then press the button with $\boxed{\text{tan}}$ written on it.

The answer 0·700 207 538 2 is displayed.

Therefore tan 35° = 0·700 207 538 2    (to 10 d.p.)

On some calculators you simply type in the expression the way it is written (i.e. $\boxed{\text{tan}}$ $\boxed{3}$ $\boxed{5}$ ). Check how your calculator works.

This result is not precisely the same as that given in the table. The result in the table is a good approximation. The result obtained from your calculator is a **very** good approximation!

(a) Use your calculator to check the values in the table.

(b) A ladder is leaning against a wall. Using the results of chapter 3, discuss if it is possible to calculate how high up the wall the ladder reaches in each of the following situations.

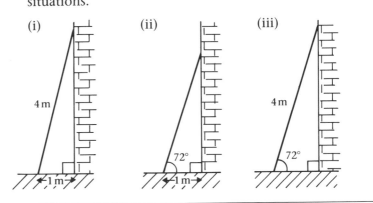

*E X A M P L E    1*

Calculate the length labelled $x$ in the diagram.

Round your answer to 2 decimal places.

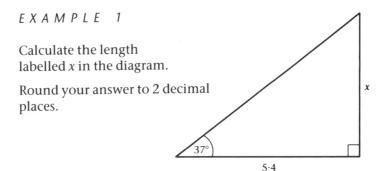

*S O L U T I O N*

$x = 5{\cdot}4 \times \tan 37°$
$\quad = 4{\cdot}069\,191 \ldots$
$\quad = 4{\cdot}07 \quad$ (to 2 d.p.)

Note that you **write** $5{\cdot}4 \times \tan 37°$ even if you have a calculator where you **type** $\boxed{5}\,\boxed{\cdot}\,\boxed{4}\,\boxed{\times}\,\boxed{3}\,\boxed{7}\,\boxed{\tan}\,\boxed{=}$ .

## 6.2 **Sin** $\theta$

Not all right-angled triangles can be solved using just tan $\theta$ and/or Pythagoras' rule. It is necessary to have a multiplier to enable you to calculate the side opposite the angle when you know the hypotenuse rather than the side adjacent to the angle. This multiplier is called the **sine** of an angle. It is usually abbreviated to **sin**.

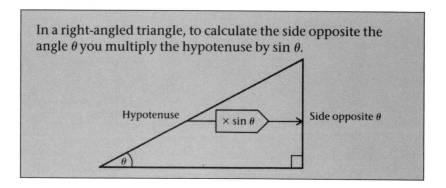

In a right-angled triangle, to calculate the side opposite the angle $\theta$ you multiply the hypotenuse by sin $\theta$.

Hypotenuse     × sin $\theta$     Side opposite $\theta$

$\theta$

You can obtain an accurate value for sin $\theta$ using the $\boxed{\text{sin}}$ button on your calculator just as you have been doing for tan $\theta$; you type in the angle, then press the button with $\boxed{\text{sin}}$ on it and the value of sin $\theta$ is displayed.

*E X A M P L E  2*

Calculate (to 2 decimal places) the length labelled $a$.

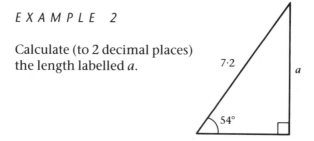

7·2

$a$

54°

*S O L U T I O N*

$a = 7{\cdot}2 \times \sin 54°$
$= 7{\cdot}2 \times 0{\cdot}80901\ldots$
$= 5{\cdot}82$ (to 2 d.p.)

On most calculators, to calculate 7·2 × sin 54° you would press keys in the following order:

$\boxed{7}\boxed{\cdot}\boxed{2}\boxed{\times}\boxed{5}\boxed{4}\boxed{\text{sin}}\boxed{=}$

On other calculators you simply enter it the way it is written.

Explain why sin $\theta$ is always a number less than 1.

### EXERCISE 1

**1** For each of these triangles, use sin $\theta$ to calculate the unknown side denoted by a letter. (Give your answer to 2 decimal places.)

(a)     (b)     (c)

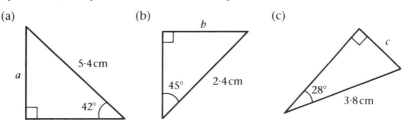

**2** For each of these triangles, first decide which angle is the appropriate one to use, then use sin $\theta$ to calculate the length marked with a letter.

(a)     (b)     (c)

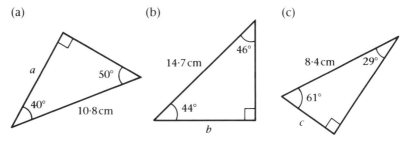

**3** A ladder which is 5·2 m long leans against a wall and makes an angle of 69° with the ground.

(a) Draw a neat sketch of a right-angled triangle to illustrate the problem. (The length and angle should be shown clearly.)

(b) Calculate how far up the wall the ladder reaches. (Round your answer to the nearest 0·01 metre.)

(c) Use Pythagoras' rule together with your answer to (b) to calculate how far the bottom of the ladder is from the wall.

(d) There is an alternative method for calculating how far the bottom of the ladder is from the wall. This method uses sin 21°. Explain carefully why the angle 21° is used and use the method to calculate the required distance. (Comment on any discrepancy between your answers.)

## 6.3 Cos θ

You have seen that the side opposite the right angle in a right-angled triangle is called the hypotenuse (hyp).

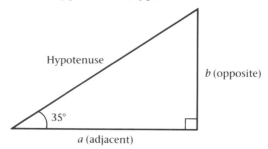

The other two sides are labelled according to where they are with respect to a particular angle (not the right angle). So with respect to the 35° angle shown in the diagram:

- *a* is the **adjacent** (adj) side because it is adjacent to (next to) the angle. (The hypotenuse is also adjacent to the angle, but it already has a special name.)

- *b* is the **opposite** (opp) side because it is opposite the angle.

However, with respect to the other angle (the 55° angle), the sides are labelled differently.

*a* is now the **opposite** side and *b* is the **adjacent** side.

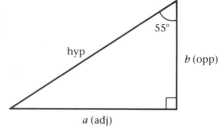

For each of the labelled sides, say if it is **opposite** or **adjacent** to the shaded angle.

(a)                    (b)                    (c)

The **cosine** of an angle (abbreviated to **cos**) is another multiplier which is useful for solving some problems.

For a right-angled triangle:

- $\text{opp} = \text{adj} \times \tan \theta$
- $\text{opp} = \text{hyp} \times \sin \theta$
- $\text{adj} = \text{hyp} \times \cos \theta$

*EXAMPLE 3*

Calculate the length $x$.
(Give your answer to
1 decimal place.)

4·7 cm

*SOLUTION*

A sketch of the triangle with the sides clearly labelled shows that a formula with 'hyp' and 'adj' is needed.

The appropriate formula is:

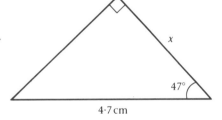

$$\text{adj} = \text{hyp} \times \cos \theta$$
$$x = 4\cdot7 \times \cos 47°$$
$$= 4\cdot7 \times 0\cdot68199\ldots$$
$$= 3\cdot2\,\text{cm} \quad (\text{to } 1 \text{ d.p.})$$

69

When solving problems using a right-angled triangle, you should:

- make a sketch showing the measurements which you are asked to find, as well as those you are given;

- label the sides hyp (hypotenuse), opp (side opposite the given angle) and adj (side adjacent to the given angle);

- decide whether to use tan, sin or cos to calculate the length asked for;

- use the appropriate formula to calculate the length.

*EXERCISE 2*

**1**  Use sin, cos or tan as appropriate to find the side asked for. (Round your answers to 2 decimal places. All dimensions are in centimetres.)

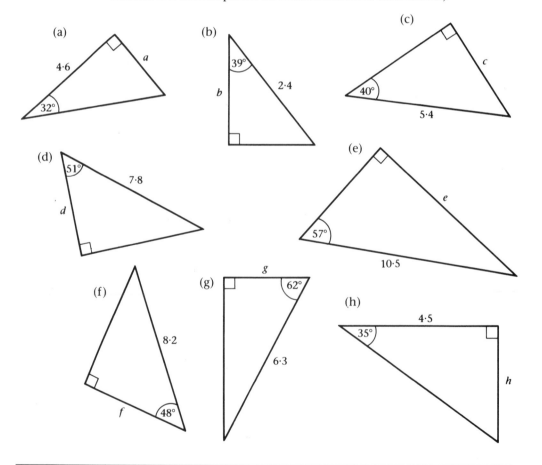

## 6.4 Calculating the hypotenuse

Instructions for erecting a short-wave radio aerial specify that each of the supporting guy-ropes should be at a 25° angle to the aerial. The guy-ropes are fixed at a height of 8 m.

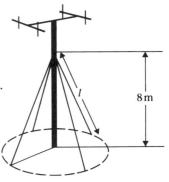

8 m

The contractor erecting the aerial has to calculate the lengths of the ropes.

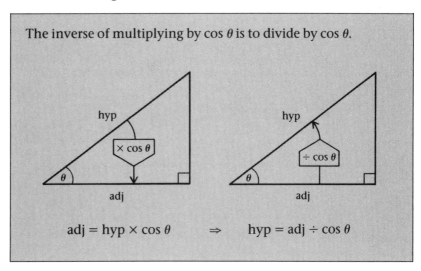

To solve this problem you sketch and label the right-angled triangle.

The appropriate formula in this situation is:

adj = hyp × cos $\theta$

Substituting into the formula gives:

8 = $l$ × cos 25°

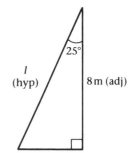

*l* (hyp)    25°    8 m (adj)

In this situation the hypotenuse is to be calculated so the formula has to be rearranged.

---

**The inverse of multiplying by cos $\theta$ is to divide by cos $\theta$.**

adj = hyp × cos $\theta$    ⇒    hyp = adj ÷ cos $\theta$

---

Use this result to calculate the lengths of the guy-ropes.

There is a similar result for sin θ.

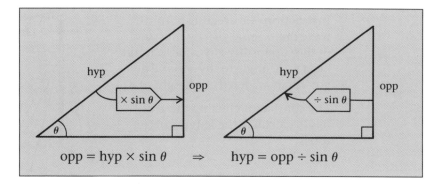

$$\text{opp} = \text{hyp} \times \sin\theta \quad \Rightarrow \quad \text{hyp} = \text{opp} \div \sin\theta$$

The questions in the next exercise are mixed. For each triangle you
must decide which of sin, cos or tan is appropriate. You must also
decide whether it is appropriate to multiply or divide. In each case,
sketch and label the right-angled triangle and show your working.

### EXERCISE 3

**1**   Find the length of each lettered side.

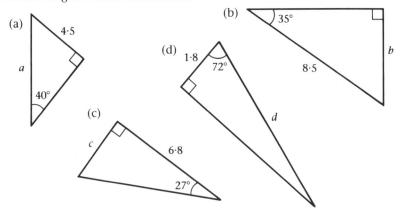

**2**   The diagram shows a roof structure. Calculate the length labelled *s*.

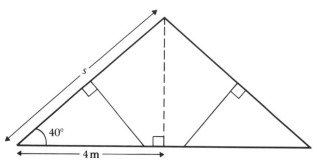

## 6.5 Calculating angles

The slope or gradient of a road is often displayed on a sign as a percentage. A 25% gradient tells you that the road increases (or decreases) 25 m vertically for every 100 m horizontally.

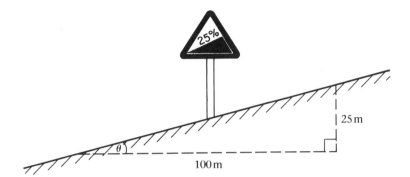

You can use this information to calculate the angle of the slope. The three basic formulas can be written as shown below.

$$\sin \theta = \frac{\text{opp}}{\text{hyp}} \qquad \cos \theta = \frac{\text{adj}}{\text{hyp}} \qquad \tan \theta = \frac{\text{opp}}{\text{hyp}}$$

Writing the formulas in this way is helpful when you have to calculate the angle.

The appropriate formula in this case is:

$$\tan \theta = \frac{\text{opp}}{\text{adj}}$$

$$= \frac{25}{100}$$

$$= 0.25$$

Find $\tan \theta$ for various angles and, by using a trial and improvement method, find a value for $\theta$ for which $\tan \theta \approx 0.25$.

The angle whose tan is 0·25 is the **inverse tangent** of 0·25. It is given the symbol **tan$^{-1}$** 0·25.

Most calculators have the symbol tan$^{-1}$ displayed above the tan button.

You can find tan$^{-1}$ 0·25 (the angle whose tan is 0·25) by entering 0·25 then pressing 2nd tan . (On some calculators you press inv tan .) On other calculators you simply enter the expression the way it is written.

> Find out how your calculator works. You should obtain the result:
>
> $$\tan^{-1} 0·25 = 14·0362\ldots°$$

Your calculator will also have inverse functions for sine (**sin$^{-1}$**) and cosine (**cos$^{-1}$**).

*E X A M P L E   4*

Find the angle $\theta$
to the nearest 0·1°.

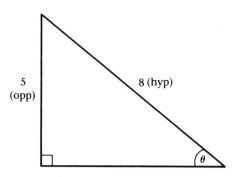

*S O L U T I O N*

The formula $\sin \theta = \dfrac{\text{opp}}{\text{hyp}}$ is appropriate here.

$\sin \theta = \frac{5}{8} = 0·625$
$\quad \theta = \sin^{-1} 0·625 \approx 38·7°$

*E X E R C I S E   4*

**1** A ladder 4 m long leans against a wall. The foot of the ladder is 1·6 m from the wall. Draw a sketch and calculate, to the nearest 0·1°, the angle that the ladder makes with the ground.

**2** Calculate, to the nearest 0·1°, the angles marked with letters in these triangles.

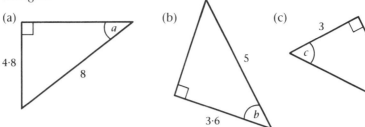

(a)

4·8

8

$a$

(b)

5

3·6

$b$

(c)

3

4

$c$

**3E** A ship leaves harbour and sails at 25 km h⁻¹. It steers for one hour on a bearing of 025° and then for two hours on a bearing of 070°.

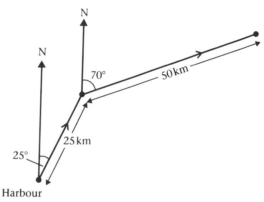

N

N

70°

50 km

25 km

25°

Harbour

Find by calculation:

(a) how far east and how far north it has travelled;

(b) its final distance and bearing from the harbour.

After working through this chapter you should:

1 understand what the terms hypotenuse, opposite and adjacent mean when labelling the sides of a right-angled triangle;

2 know the trigonometric relationships:

- opp = hyp × sin $\theta$
- adj = hyp × cos $\theta$
- opp = adj × tan $\theta$

and how to use a calculator to evaluate them;

3 know how to calculate an angle in a right-angled triangle using inverse sine, cosine or tangent.

# Solutions

## 1 Positions and polygons

### 1.1 Loci

*EXERCISE 1*

For convenience, the answers to this exercise have been drawn to a reduced scale.

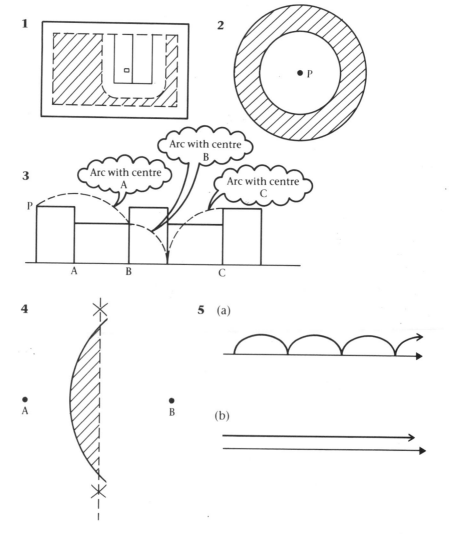

## 1.2   Polygons

(a) Use the method of example 3 to find the sums of the interior angles of polygons with 5, 6 and 7 sides. Then copy and complete the table.

| Name of polygon | Number of sides | Sum of angles (°) |
|---|---|---|
| Triangle | 3 | 180 |
| Quadrilateral | 4 | 360 |
| Pentagon | 5 | |
| Hexagon | 6 | |
| Heptagon | 7 | |
| Octagon | 8 | 1080 |

(b) Describe the pattern in the sequence of numbers in the last column.

(c) Extend the table to include the nonagon (9 sides) and the decagon (10 sides).

(a)

| Name of polygon | Number of sides | Sum of angles (°) |
|---|---|---|
| Triangle | 3 | 180 |
| Quadrilateral | 4 | 360 |
| Pentagon | 5 | 540 |
| Hexagon | 6 | 720 |
| Heptagon | 7 | 900 |
| Octagon | 8 | 1080 |

(b) The sum of the angles increases by 180° from each row to the next.

(c)

| | | |
|---|---|---|
| Nonagon | 9 | 1260 |
| Decagon | 10 | 1440 |

EXERCISE 2

**1**  (a) He turns through 40° at A.

(b) At D he has turned through 40° + 50° + 80° = 170°.

(c) He must turn through 360° − (170° + 100°) = 90°.

## 1.3 Regular polygons

(a) Sketch a regular heptagon. (You can use a 50p coin to fix the corners and then use a ruler to join them.) On your sketch, draw in dashed lines to show the lines of symmetry.

(b) Write down the order of rotational symmetry. (The order of rotational symmetry is the number of times a shape fits onto its original position as it is rotated through 360°.)

(c) What name is given to a regular polygon with:

    (i) 3 sides;    (ii) 4 sides?

(d) Describe the symmetry of these polygons.

(a)

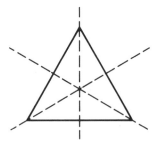

(b) Rotational symmetry order 7

(c) (i) Equilateral triangle    (ii) Square

(d) An equilateral triangle
has three lines of symmetry
and rotational symmetry order 3.

A square has four lines of
symmetry and rotational
symmetry order 4.

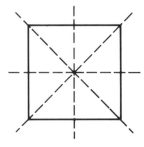

(a) On a sketch of a regular hexagon, draw in dashed lines to show the lines of symmetry and state the order of rotational symmetry.

(b) How many lines of symmetry has a regular polygon with $n$ sides?

(c) What can you say about the rotational symmetry of such a polygon?

(d) Draw hexagons which are **not** regular and yet have:

  (i) equal sides;    (ii) equal angles.

(a) Rotational symmetry order 6

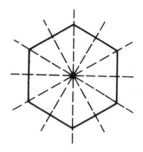

(b) There are $n$ lines of symmetry.

(c) It has rotational symmetry order $n$.

(d) (i)                                    (ii)

There are many other possible answers.

*E X E R C I S E  3*

1  The exterior angle is $360° ÷ 10 = 36°$.
  The interior angle is $180° − 36° = 144°$.

2  (a) Angle AOB $= 360° ÷ 8 = 45°$.

  (b) Angle BAF $= 90°$. You can see that this is so by symmetry.

**3**

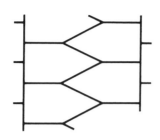

# 2 Directions

## 2.1 Bearings

> A passenger in the balloon looks back to the point of take-off and uses a compass to take a bearing.
>
> What bearing does her compass show?

$180° + 54° = 234°$

## 2.2 Fixing a position

> How can you fix the position of the tower?

Lines drawn in the directions of the measured bearings fix the position where they cross. This method is called triangulation and is used in tasksheet 1.

*E X E R C I S E  1*

**1**  The feature is a caravan site near Barber Booth, GR 117849.

**2**

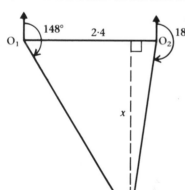

$x = 3·1$
The boat is 3·1 km from the shore.

**3**

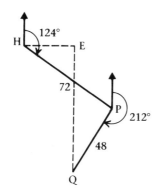

(a) HE = 34
EQ = 81
The ship has travelled 34 km east and 81 km south.

(b) The ship is 88 km from harbour, on a bearing of 157°.

## 2.3 Vectors

> Describe this journey using a distance and a bearing.

AB is about 2·4 ÷ 4 = 0·6 km. The bearing of B from A is 059°.

> If M is at GR 192858 and N is at GR 197851 write the vector $\overrightarrow{MN}$ in terms of distance along the ground.

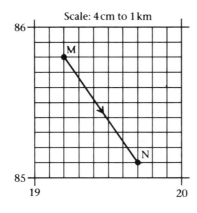

$$\overrightarrow{MN} = \begin{bmatrix} 5 \\ -7 \end{bmatrix} \text{ grid squares}$$

$$= \begin{bmatrix} 0·5 \\ -0·7 \end{bmatrix} \text{ km}$$

> In example 1, write down the vector $\overrightarrow{QP}$.

$$\overrightarrow{QP} = \begin{bmatrix} 3 \\ -5 \end{bmatrix}$$

> Write down the translation vector which sends the flag from:
>
> (a) $F_1$ to $F_2$     (b) $F_2$ to $F_1$     (c) $F_1$ to $F_3$
>
> (d) $F_3$ to $F_1$     (e) $F_2$ to $F_3$     (f) $F_3$ to $F_2$

(a) $\overrightarrow{F_1F_2} = \begin{bmatrix} 10 \\ {-3} \end{bmatrix}$  (b) $\overrightarrow{F_2F_1} = \begin{bmatrix} {-10} \\ 3 \end{bmatrix}$

(c) $\overrightarrow{F_1F_3} = \begin{bmatrix} 4 \\ {-9} \end{bmatrix}$  (d) $\overrightarrow{F_3F_1} = \begin{bmatrix} {-4} \\ 9 \end{bmatrix}$

(e) $\overrightarrow{F_2F_3} = \begin{bmatrix} {-6} \\ {-6} \end{bmatrix}$  (f) $\overrightarrow{F_3F_2} = \begin{bmatrix} 6 \\ 6 \end{bmatrix}$

---

Write down the coordinates of:

(a)  the mid-point of AB;

(b)  the mid-point of OC.

---

(a)  $(30, 20, 50)$    (b)  $(0, 20, 25)$

---

Copy both of the sets of axes illustrated and on each one show the point $(30, 40, 50)$ using a dashed cuboid as on the previous page.

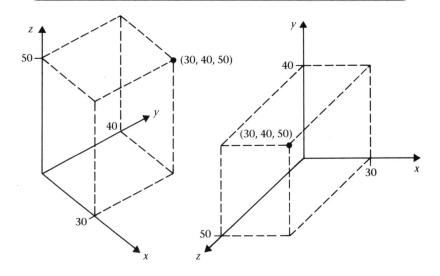

# 3  Right-angled triangles

## 3.1  Pythagoras' rule

Show how this dissection enables you to calculate the area of the large square.

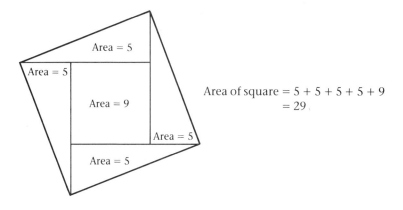

Area of square $= 5 + 5 + 5 + 5 + 9$
$= 29$

*E X E R C I S E   1*

**1**　(a)　$A = 3^2 + 4^2 = 25$ square units　　(b)　$A = 13^2 - 5^2 = 144$ square units

　　(c)　$A = 13^2 + 5^2 = 194$ square units

**2**　(a)　You cannot use Pythagoras' rule for (ii) as it is not a right-angled triangle.

　　(b)　(i)　$x^2 = 3^2 + 6^2 \Rightarrow x = \sqrt{45} = 6{\cdot}71$　(to 2 d.p.)

　　　　(iii)　$z^2 = 8^2 - 5^2 \Rightarrow z = \sqrt{39} = 6{\cdot}24$　(to 2 d.p.)

**3**　(a)　$l^2 = 3^2 + 5^2 \Rightarrow l = \sqrt{34} = 5{\cdot}83$　(to 2 d.p.)

　　(b)　$l^2 = 3^2 + 3^2 \Rightarrow l = \sqrt{18} = 4{\cdot}24$　(to 2 d.p.)

　　(c)　$l^2 = 1^2 + 5^2 \Rightarrow l = \sqrt{26} = 5{\cdot}10$　(to 2 d.p.)

**4**　$l^2 = 250^2 + 600^2 \Rightarrow l = \sqrt{422\,500} = 650$
Each rope is 650 cm long.

## 3.2　Pythagorean triples

(a)　How do you know that a triangle with sides of length 3, 4 and 5 must be a right-angled triangle?

The following table shows some Pythagorean triples.

| $a$ | $b$ | $c$ |
|---|---|---|
| 3 | 4 | 5 |
| 5 | 12 | 13 |
| 7 | 24 | 25 |

(b)　Use Pythagoras' rule to check the values given in the table.

(c)　Find at least one other Pythagorean triple.

(a) The area of the square on the longest side, $5^2$, is equal to the sum of the areas of the squares on the other two sides ($5^2 = 3^2 + 4^2$). This relationship is only true for right-angled triangles.

(b) $3^2 + 4^2 = 9 + 16 = 25 = 5^2$
$5^2 + 12^2 = 25 + 144 = 169 = 13^2$
$7^2 + 24^2 = 49 + 576 = 625 = 25^2$

(c) There are many possible answers. Some possibilities are:

$$(9, 40, 41), \quad (11, 60, 61), \quad (13, 84, 85)$$

You are likely to have found a smaller triple, such as $(6, 8, 10)$ or $(9, 12, 15)$. Note that these are simple multiples of the $(3, 4, 5)$ triple.

---

Calculate the enlargement scale factor used to transform:

(a) triangle $Q$ to triangle $R$;

(b) triangle $Q$ to triangle $P$;

(c) triangle $P$ to triangle $R$.

---

(a) 3 (All equivalent lengths are 3 times as long.)

(b) $\frac{1}{2}$ (All equivalent lengths are $\frac{1}{2}$ as long.)

(c) 6 (All equivalent lengths are 6 times as long.)

## 3.3 The tangent of an angle

---

Accurately construct a 35° right-angled triangle of your own choice and show that, whatever size triangle you choose, it is always true that $a \times 0{\cdot}7 = b$.

---

You will find that $a \times 0{\cdot}7 = b$ for any 35° right-angled triangle when you allow for inaccuracies in measurements.

---

(a) For what angle $\theta$ does $\tan \theta = 1$?

(b) What is the value of $\tan 0°$?

(c) Why is $\tan 90°$ not shown in the table?

(a) tan $\theta$ = 1 when $\theta$ = 45°    (b) tan 0° = 0

(c) When $\theta$ = 90°, the tangent and the radius are parallel and so tan 90° does not have a value.

*E X E R C I S E   2*

**1**  (a) $a$ =  5 tan 50° =   5 × 1·192 = 5·96   (to 2 d.p.)

(b) $b$ =  7 tan 40° =   7 × 0·839 = 5·87   (to 2 d.p.)

(c) $c$ = 10 tan 20° = 10 × 0·364 = 3·64   (to 2 d.p.)

**2**  (a) $a$ =  4 tan 60° =   4 × 1·732 = 6·93   (to 2 d.p.)

(b) $b$ = 20 tan 45° = 20 × 1 = 20

(c) $c$ =  3 tan 80° =   3 × 5·671 = 17·01   (to 2 d.p.)

**3**  (a) $\tan \theta = \frac{5}{7}$  ≈ 0·714; $\theta$ is just over 35°.

(b) $\tan \theta = \frac{4}{11}$ ≈ 0·364; $\theta$ is very close to 20°.

(c) $\tan \theta = \frac{12}{7}$ ≈ 1·714; $\theta$ is nearly 60°.

**4**

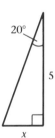

$x$ = 5 tan 20°
  = 5 × 0·364
The foot of the ladder is 1·82 metres from the building.

# 4 Perimeters and areas

## 4.1  Circumference of a circle

(a) How accurate is the approximation $\pi \approx \frac{22}{7}$ ?

(b) For each of these circles, calculate the circumference, first by doing a mental calculation using $\pi \approx 3$, and then by using your calculator to obtain an accurate solution.

(i)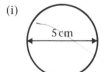

(ii)

(a) The two numbers agree to 2 decimal places. If you take 3 decimal places then $\pi \approx 3.142$ but $\frac{22}{7} \approx 3.143$.

(b) (i) $c \approx 3 \times 5 = 15$ cm

$c = \pi \times 5 = 15.708$ cm   (to 3 d.p.)

(ii) $c \approx 2 \times 3 \times 5 = 30$ m

$c = 2 \times \pi \times 5 = 31.416$ m

(to 3 d.p.)

## EXERCISE 1

**1** –

**2** (a) The diameter is about $18 \div 3 = 6$ cm.

(b) It is $18 \div \pi = 5.73$ cm to 2 decimal places.

**3** The length of strip needed is $2 \times \pi \times 80 = 503$ cm to the nearest centimetre.

**4** (a) The distance travelled in one turn is $\pi \times 70 \approx 220$ cm or 2·2 m.

(b) The number of turns in 2 km is $2000 \div 2.2 \approx 900$.

## 4.2   Area of a circle

Explain why the area of the circle is:

- smaller than $4r^2$;
- larger than $2r^2$.

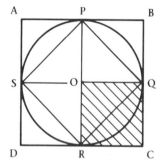

The shaded area is $r \times r = r^2$.
So the area of ABCD is $4r^2$.
QR divides the shaded area in half, so the area of triangle OQR is $\frac{1}{2}r^2$.
Hence the area of PQRS is $4 \times \frac{1}{2}r^2 = 2r^2$.
The area of the circle lies between the area of ABCD and the area of PQRS and so is smaller than $4r^2$ but greater than $2r^2$.

How much card would be wasted?

The area of card is $15 \times 10 = 150$ cm$^2$.
The area of the circle is $78.5$ cm$^2$.
So the area wasted is $150 - 78.5 = 71.5$ cm$^2$.

*E X E R C I S E   2*

**1**   (a)  62·8 cm;   314·2 cm²     (b)  24·5 cm;   47·8 cm²

(c)  88·0 cm;   615·8 cm²

**2**   (a)  19·5 + 12·4 = 31·9 cm;   60·4 cm²

(b)  $\frac{3}{4}$ × 36·4 + 2 × 5·8 = 38·9 cm;   $\frac{3}{4}$ × 105·7 = 79·3 cm²

**3**   Six discs can be stamped out, with area 6 × $\pi$ × 4² = 302 cm².
The area of the sheet is 413 cm², so the wastage is approximately 110 cm².

**4**   (a)  $r \approx \sqrt{(12 \div 3)}$ = 2 cm

(b)  $r = \sqrt{(12 \div \pi)}$ = 1·95 cm    (to 2 d.p.)

**5E**   The area of the target is 7854 cm², so the area of the bull's-eye is 78·5 cm².
Hence the radius of the bull's-eye is $\sqrt{(78·54 \div \pi)}$ = 5·00 cm. So the
diameter is 10 cm.

## 4.3   **The parallelogram**

> Describe the symmetry properties of a parallelogram.

There are **no** lines of reflection symmetry.
There is rotational symmetry of order 2.

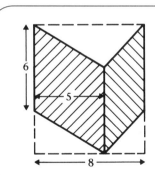

The total shaded area consists of two
parallelograms 'back to back'.
(Dimensions are in cm.) Find the area.

The area of the left-hand parallelogram is 6 × 5 = 30 cm².
The area of the right-hand parallelogram is 6 × 3 = 18 cm².
The total area is 48 cm².

Describe how the diagonals of a
rhombus cross.

They bisect each other at right angles.

*E X E R C I S E  3*

**1**  (a)  $6.3 \times 4.2 = 26.5 \,\text{cm}^2$  (to 1 d.p.)  (b)  $1.2 \times 2.5 = 3 \,\text{cm}^2$

**2**  (a)  $5.6 \times 4.8 = 26.9 \,\text{cm}^2$  (to 1 d.p.)  (b)  $5.0 \times 6.8 = 34 \,\text{cm}^2$

## 4.4  The trapezium

(a)  What type of quadrilateral is the combined shape?

(b)  Explain why the area of each trapezium is $\frac{1}{2}(a + b)h$.

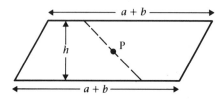

(a)  The two trapeziums form a parallelogram. The area of the parallelogram is $(a + b) \times h$.

(b)  Each trapezium is a half of the parallelogram.

Sketch an isosceles trapezium, mark on its line of symmetry, and show clearly which angles are equal.

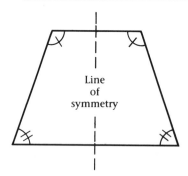

Line of symmetry

*E X E R C I S E  4*

**1**  (a)  $\frac{1}{2}(5 + 8) \times 4 = 26 \,\text{cm}^2$  (b)  $\frac{1}{2}(7.2 + 4.8) \times 4.2 = 25.2 \,\text{cm}^2$

(c)  $\frac{1}{2}(5.6 + 3.1) \times 4.8 = 20.9 \,\text{cm}^2$  (to 1 d.p.)

**2**  The average of the parallel sides is $3.85 \,\text{cm}$. So the distance between them is $\dfrac{9.2}{3.85} = 2.39 \,\text{cm}$  (to 2 d.p.).

**3**

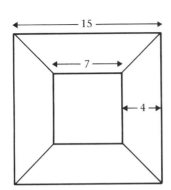

**Method 1**

The distance between the sides of the square is:

$$\frac{15 - 7}{2} = 4\,\text{cm}$$

The area is $\frac{1}{2}(15 + 7) \times 4 = 44\,\text{cm}^2$.

**Method 2**

The area of the large square is $15^2 = 225\,\text{cm}^2$.
The area of the small square is $7^2 = 49\,\text{cm}^2$.
The area of the four trapeziums is $225 - 49 = 176\,\text{cm}^2$.
So the area of each trapezium is $\frac{176}{4} = 44\,\text{cm}^2$.

**4** (a) The area of the roof is:

$$2 \times \tfrac{1}{2}(5 + 11) \times 3{\cdot}6 + 2 \times \tfrac{1}{2} \times 6 \times 3{\cdot}6 = 79{\cdot}2\,\text{m}^2$$

(b) The cost is $79{\cdot}2 \times £20 = £1584$.

## 4.5 Classifying quadrilaterals

> Look at the diagram and answer these questions.
>
> (a) Is a rectangle a parallelogram?
>
> (b) Is a parallelogram a rectangle?

(a) Yes, it is a right-angled parallelogram.

(b) Not necessarily. It is a rectangle only if it has a right angle.

## 4.6 Composite shapes

> (a) Find the area of the shape illustrated by considering it to be made from two simpler shapes.
>
> (b) Find the area of the shape illustrated by considering it to be a larger shape with a section removed.

(a)

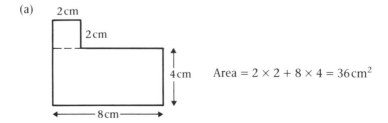

Area $= 2 \times 2 + 8 \times 4 = 36\,\text{cm}^2$

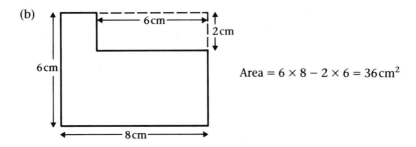

(b)

Area = $6 \times 8 - 2 \times 6 = 36\,\text{cm}^2$

*EXERCISE 5*

**1** (a) The area is $\frac{1}{2}(5 + 9) \times 4 = 28\,\text{cm}^2$.

   (b) The area is $2 \times 6 + 2 \times 8 = 28\,\text{cm}^2$.

**2** The areas are: Bull's-eye $\quad \pi\,\text{cm}^2 \approx 3\cdot14\,\text{cm}^2$
   Inner $\quad 4\pi - \pi = 3\pi \approx 9\cdot42\,\text{cm}^2$
   Magpie $\quad 9\pi - 4\pi = 5\pi \approx 15\cdot71\,\text{cm}^2$
   Outer $\quad 16\pi - 9\pi = 7\pi \approx 21\cdot99\,\text{cm}^2$

**3** (a) $\pi \times 1^2 + 2 \times 3 = 9\cdot14\,\text{m}^2$ (to 2 d.p.)

   (b) $4 \times 4 - \pi \times 2^2 = 3\cdot43\,\text{m}^2$ (to 2 d.p.)

**4E** (a) The shaded area is $5 \times 5 - \frac{1}{4}(\pi \times 5^2) = 5\cdot37\,\text{cm}^2$ (to 2 d.p.).

   (b) The shaded area is $25 - 2 \times 5\cdot37 = 14\cdot3\,\text{cm}^2$ (to 1 d.p.).

# 5 Three-dimensional shapes

## 5.2 Prisms

*EXERCISE 1*

**1** The volume is $20 \times 15 \times 0\cdot6 = 180\,\text{cm}^3$.

**2** The area of cross-section is $\pi \times (3\cdot2)^2 \approx 32\,\text{cm}^2$.
   The volume is $32 \times 0\cdot4 \approx 13\,\text{cm}^3$.

**3** The area of cross-section is $\frac{1}{4} \times \pi \times 1^2 \approx 0\cdot79\,\text{cm}^2$.
   The volume is $0\cdot79 \times 200 \approx 160\,\text{cm}^3$.

**4** The cross-section is a trapezium of area $\frac{1}{2}(2\cdot4 + 3\cdot0) \times 2\cdot4 = 6\cdot48\,\text{m}^2$.
   The volume is $6\cdot48 \times 3\cdot6 \approx 23\,\text{m}^3$.
   Two candles are enough.

## 5.3 Nets

(a) Calculate the area of the net.

(b) Sketch two other possible nets for the same triangular prism.

(a)

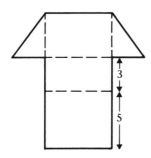

The net could be dissected and reassembled like this. Its area is:

$$(6 \times 12) + (3 \times 4) = 84 \, \text{cm}^2$$

(b) Two alternatives are shown below. There are others.

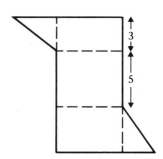

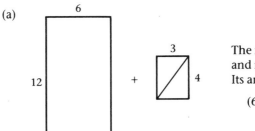

*EXERCISE 2*

**1** (a) 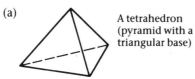 A tetrahedron (pyramid with a triangular base)

(b) A pyramid with a square base

**2** (a)

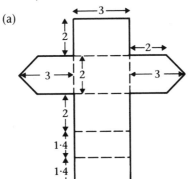 Many other answers are possible.

91

(b) Each end wall can be thought of as a square and a triangle.

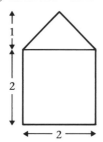

Each has area:

$$2 \times 2 + \tfrac{1}{2} \times 2 \times 1 = 5\,\text{m}^2$$

The total area is:

$$2 \times 5 + 3 \times (2 + 2 + 2 + 1\cdot4 + 1\cdot4) = 36\cdot4\,\text{m}^2$$

(c) The interior of the shed has the form of a prism.
The area of cross-section is $(2 \times 2) + (\tfrac{1}{2} \times 2 \times 1) = 5\,\text{m}^2$.
The volume is $5 \times 3 = 15\,\text{m}^3$.

**3** (a) The solid is a hexagonal prism. The shape of each missing end-face is a regular hexagon.

(b) The second face could be at any one of the six possible positions on the right side of the rectangle. A possible net is illustrated.

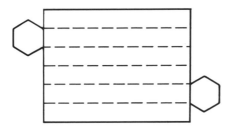

**4E** (a)

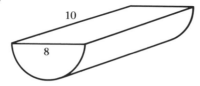

(b)

$$x = \tfrac{1}{2} \times (\pi \times 8)$$
$$= 12\cdot6 \quad \text{(to 1 d.p.)}$$

(c) The area of cross-section is $\tfrac{1}{2} \times \pi \times 4^2 \approx 25\,\text{cm}^2$.
The volume is $25 \times 10 = 250\,\text{cm}^3$.

(d)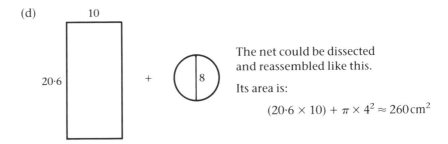

The net could be dissected and reassembled like this.

Its area is:

$$(20.6 \times 10) + \pi \times 4^2 \approx 260\,\text{cm}^2$$

## 5.4 Dimensions

> What do these formulas stand for?

A circle of radius $r$ has circumference (a **length**) $2\pi r$ and **area** $\pi r^2$.

> A student uses the formula $\frac{2}{3}\pi r^2$ for the volume of a hemisphere. Why must she be mistaken?

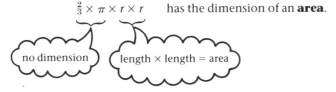

$\frac{2}{3} \times \pi \times r \times r$  has the dimension of an **area**.

no dimension

length × length = area

The formula for the **volume** of a hemisphere is $\frac{2}{3}\pi r^3$.

# 6 Trigonometry

## 6.2 Sin $\theta$

> Explain why sin $\theta$ is always a number less than 1.

The side opposite the angle must be shorter than the hypotenuse so the multiplier must be less than 1.

*EXERCISE 1*

**1** (a) $a = 5\cdot4 \times \sin 42° = 5\cdot4 \times 0\cdot669\ldots = 3\cdot61\,\text{cm}$   (to 2 d.p.)

   (b) $b = 2\cdot4 \times \sin 45° = 2\cdot4 \times 0\cdot707\ldots = 1\cdot70\,\text{cm}$   (to 2 d.p.)

   (c) $c = 3\cdot8 \times \sin 28° = 3\cdot8 \times 0\cdot469\ldots = 1\cdot78\,\text{cm}$   (to 2 d.p.)

**2** (a) $a = 10\cdot8 \times \sin 50° = 8\cdot27\,\text{cm}$   (to 2 d.p.)

   (b) $b = 14\cdot7 \times \sin 46° = 10\cdot57\,\text{cm}$   (to 2 d.p.)

   (c) $c = \phantom{0}8\cdot4 \times \sin 29° = 4\cdot07\,\text{cm}$   (to 2 d.p.)

**3** (a)

```
         /|
     5·2/ |
      /   | h
     /    |
    /69°  |
   /_____|
      d
```

   (b) $h = 5\cdot2 \times \sin 69° \approx 4\cdot85\,\text{m}$

   (c) $d^2 = 5\cdot2^2 - 4\cdot85^2 = 3\cdot5175$
      $d \approx 1\cdot88\,\text{m}$

   (d) The angles of a triangle add up to 180°. As two of the angles are known to be 90° and 69°, the angle the ladder makes with the wall must be $180 - (90 + 69) = 21°$. The distance, $d$, is opposite this angle so $d = 5\cdot2 \times \sin 21°$.

   $$d = 5\cdot2 \times \sin 21° \approx 1\cdot86\,\text{m}$$

   The discrepancy is due to rounding the answer to (b). $d = 1\cdot86\,\text{m}$ is more accurate.

### 6.3   Cos $\theta$

For each of the labelled sides, say if it is **opposite** or **adjacent** to the shaded angle.

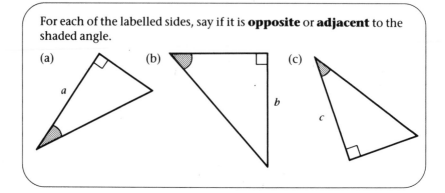

(a)     (b)     (c)

(a) Adjacent     (b) Opposite     (c) Adjacent

*E X E R C I S E   2*

**1**  (a)  $a = 4{\cdot}6 \times \tan 32° \approx 2{\cdot}87\,\text{cm}$    (b)  $b = 2{\cdot}4 \times \cos 39° \approx 1{\cdot}87\,\text{cm}$

(c)  $c = 5{\cdot}4 \times \sin 40° \approx 3{\cdot}47\,\text{cm}$    (d)  $d = 7{\cdot}8 \times \cos 51° \approx 4{\cdot}91\,\text{cm}$

(e)  $e = 10{\cdot}5 \times \sin 57° \approx 8{\cdot}81\,\text{cm}$    (f)  $f = 8{\cdot}2 \times \cos 48° \approx 5{\cdot}49\,\text{cm}$

(g)  $g = 6{\cdot}3 \times \cos 62° \approx 2{\cdot}96\,\text{cm}$    (h)  $h = 4{\cdot}5 \times \tan 35° \approx 3{\cdot}15\,\text{cm}$

## 6.4  Calculating the hypotenuse

> Use this result to calculate the lengths of the guy-ropes.

$l = 8 \div \cos 25°$
$\quad = 8 \div 0{\cdot}906 \ldots$
$\quad = 8{\cdot}827 \ldots \text{m}$   (8·83 m would be a suitable rounding.)

*E X E R C I S E   3*

**1**  (a)  $4{\cdot}5 = a \times \sin 40°$
$\quad\quad a = 4{\cdot}5 \div \sin 40°$
$\quad\quad\quad = 7{\cdot}00$   (to 2 d.p.)

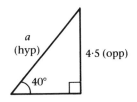

(b)  $b = 8{\cdot}5 \times \sin 35°$
$\quad\quad = 4{\cdot}88$   (to 2 d.p.)

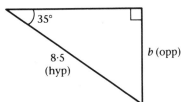

(c)  $c = 6{\cdot}8 \times \tan 27°$
$\quad\quad = 3{\cdot}46$   (to 2 d.p.)

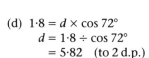

(d)  $1{\cdot}8 = d \times \cos 72°$
$\quad\quad d = 1{\cdot}8 \div \cos 72°$
$\quad\quad\quad = 5{\cdot}82$   (to 2 d.p.)

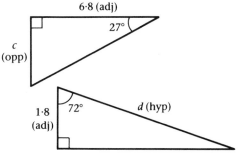

**2**

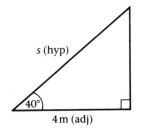

$s \times \cos 40° = 4$
$s = 4 \div \cos 40°$
$\quad = 5{\cdot}22\,\text{m}$   (to 2 d.p.)

### 6.5   Calculating angles

> Find tan $\theta$ for various angles and, by using a trial and improvement method, find a value for $\theta$ for which tan $\theta \approx 0.25$.

The angle is between 14° and 14·5°.

> Find out how your calculator works. You should obtain the result:
>
> $\tan^{-1} 0.25 = 14.0362\ldots°$

If you do not get this result, ask your teacher for help.

*EXERCISE 4*

**1**

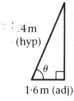

$4 \times \cos \theta = 1.6$

$\cos \theta = 0.4$

$\theta = \cos^{-1} 0.4$

$\approx 66.4°$

**2**   (a) $a = \sin^{-1} 0.6 \approx 36.9°$   (b) $b = \cos^{-1} 0.72 \approx 43.9°$

(c) $c = \tan^{-1} 1.333\ldots \approx 53.1°$

**3E**   (a) **1st stage**

Distance north $= 25 \cos 25°$
$\qquad\qquad\quad = 22.66\,\text{km}$   (to 2 d.p.)

Distance east $\;= 25 \sin 25°$
$\qquad\qquad\quad = 10.57\,\text{km}$   (to 2 d.p.)

**2nd stage**

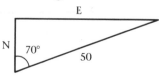

Distance north $= 50 \cos 70°$
$\qquad\qquad\quad = 17.10\,\text{km}$   (to 2 d.p.)

Distance east $\;= 50 \sin 70°$
$\qquad\qquad\quad = 46.98\,\text{km}$   (to 2 d.p.)

The total distance north is $22.66 + 17.10 = 39.76\,\text{km}$.
The total distance east is   $10.57 + 46.98 = 57.55\,\text{km}$.

(b)

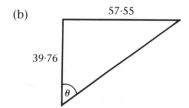

Total distance $= \sqrt{(39.76^2 + 57.55^2)}$
$\qquad\qquad\quad = 69.95\,\text{km}$   (to 2 d.p.)

Bearing $= \tan^{-1}(57.55 \div 39.76)$
$\qquad\quad = 055.4°$   (to 1 d.p.)